THE TREASURE
OF MY CATHOLIC FAITH

 NATIONAL CONSULTANTS FOR EDUCATION, INC.

CIRCLE
PRESS
SCHOLASTIC

BOOK DESIGN   PPA Media

ILLUSTRATIONS   Dolores Cortes, Edmundo Santamaria.

"The Ad Hoc Committee to Oversee the Use of the Catechism, United States Conference of Catholic Bishops, has found this catechetical text, copyright 2003, to be in conformity with the *Catechism of the Catholic Church*."

ISBN 0-9743661-4-5

Anima Christi taken from "Catholic Household Blessings & Prayers"
© 1989 United States Conference of Catholic Bishops

Act of Faith, Hope and Love & Eucharistic Hour Prayer taken from
"The Handbook of Indulgences Norms & Grants"
© 1991 Catholic Book Publishing Co.

Psalm 8 taken from "The New American Bible"
© 1987 Catholic Book Publishing Co.

Printed in the United States of America

Published by Circle Press Scholastic, an imprint of Circle Press, a division of Circle Media, Inc.
For more information or to purchase this title contact:
Circle Press
PO Box 5425
Hamden, CT 06518-0425
www.catholictextbooks.org
888-881-0729

CONTENTS

God Created Everything Out of Love

Hey there! We're apostles of Jesus! We're going to come along with you to tell you about Jesus so that you can get to be one of his best friends, just like us!

When we used to go walking with Jesus, traveling far and wide from town to town, he liked to stop on the way to watch the birds of the air and smell the flowers of the fields, just like you do. Why do you think God created everything we see around us?

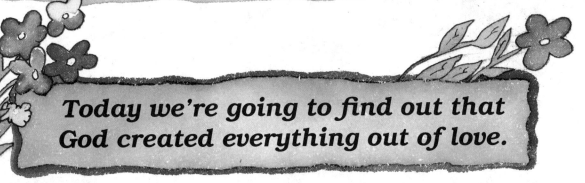

Today we're going to find out that God created everything out of love.

Do you remember how God created the world?

1. On the first day, God created day and night, separating light from darkness.
2. On the second day he created the earth and the sky.
3. On the third day he made the rivers, the lakes, and the oceans, separating the waters from the dry land. He also made the trees and plants.
4. On the fourth day he created the stars, the comets, and all the heavenly bodies of the universe.
5. On the fifth day he made all the animals of the earth and all the fish of the sea.
6. On the sixth day, God created the most important part of creation: man and woman.

Look at the drawing and answer the questions.

Find a fish jumping out of the water.
What day did God create the fish?_____
Find a red flower.
What day did God create the plants and flowers?_____
Find a red cap and a girl in a red dress.
What day did God create humans? _____
Find a shooting star.
What day did God create the stars? _____
Find the sun.
What day did God create the day and the night? _____
Find some drops of water.
What day did God create the oceans?_____

God created everything for a reason

All of creation has a purpose. God created it for a special reason.

Fill in the blanks.

exists - loves - God - happy

_____ created everything that

_____ because he

_____ us and wants us

to be _____.

Write a little story that goes with the pictures.

_____   _____   _____
_____   _____   _____
_____   _____   _____
_____   _____   _____
_____   _____   _____

Respond:

What did the mother do?

_____

Who did she do it for?

_____

Why did she do it?

_____

That's just how it is with God and creation: God created everything because he loves us very much and wants us to be happy.

Draw three things from creation that make you happy, and then write why they make you happy.

This is a drawing of _____
It makes me happy because:
_____
_____

This is a drawing of _____
It makes me happy because:
_____
_____

This is a drawing of _____
It makes me happy because:
_____

_____

Creation is a beautiful gift God has given us.
What do you do when someone gives you a gift?

Draw a blue line under the answers that seem right to you:

• **Feel happy**

• **Ignore it**

• **Say "thank you!"**

• **Take good care of it**

God has given you a lot of wonderful gifts in creation. How are you going to thank him for them?

Go to the school chapel and thank him for everything he's given you.

Do this crossword puzzle.

1 across: What did God create on the second day, together with the sky?
2 down: What did God create on the fourth day?
3 across: God created everything because he _____ us.
4 down: God also created everything because he wants us to be...

What I have learned

- God created everything that exists, visible and invisible.
- God created everything because he loves us and wants us to be happy.
- Creation is a wonderful gift from God and we should thank him for it and take good care of it.

What I will always remember

Who created everything that exists?
God created everything that exists.

What did God create?
God created everything that exists, visible and invisible.

Why did God create everything that exists?
God created because he loves us and wants us to be happy.

What I am going to do

- I'm going to thank God for the great gift of creation and for how much he loves me.
- By taking good care of the wonderful gift of creation, I'm going to show God that I love him.

God Made Us Different

Take a careful look at everything around you.
Rocks are very different from plants,
cats don't look at all like birds,
and the sun is very different from the clouds.

We are also very different from the rest of creation.
God has created us in a very special way.

**Today we are going to learn that God
has given us a very special kind of life.**

Look at how we were created

God saved the last day of creation for something very special. When he had already made everything else in the universe: the earth and the sky, the plants and the animals; God took some clay from the earth and shaped it into a man.

Then he breathed into him to give him a special kind of life, one he didn't give to anything else in creation.

Color this picture.

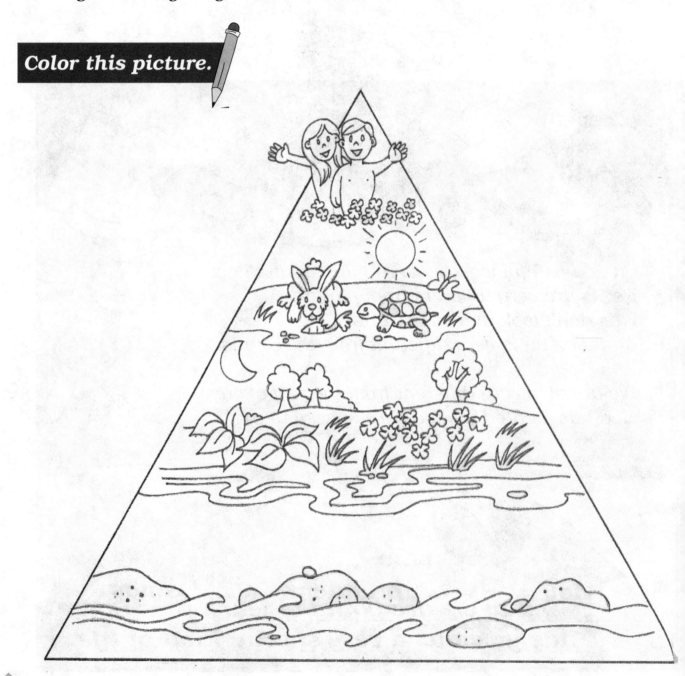

Discover the most important part of creation.

Look at the puzzle below. Redraw the pictures in the boxes below. Put each box in its correct place by following the numbers.

People have a very special place in creation. God created us with a very special love.

1	2	3
4	5	6
7	8	9

God has created us with special love

God has made us very special. We are different from all the rest of creation.

God created us in his own image and likeness. He made us to be like himself.

God has given us a body and a soul.

So we are able to know and love God.

See these children? They are looking at themselves in the mirror.

Draw them in the mirror.

We are images of God because he has made us in a special way. He not only gave us bodies, but gave us souls too, creating us in his own image and likeness.

God has given us a special kind of life

**This life means having God in our souls.
It is called the "life of grace."
We receive the life of grace on the day of our baptism
by the working of the Holy Spirit.**

What is "grace"?

- Grace is a participation in the life of the Blessed Trinity
- Grace makes us participate in the grace of Christ and in the Holy Spirit, so as to be "adopted" sons of the Father

Find these words and phrases in this alphabet soup:

Life of Grace - knowing God - loving God - gift
help - heaven - image - soul

U	M	J	D	A	T	L	O	V	I	N	G	G	O	D
O	R	H	E	L	P	D	S	R	W	S	V	L	I	R
P	F	R	D	A	F	O	H	E	A	V	E	N	M	R
B	E	S	I	W	E	I	L	V	L	N	E	L	D	V
T	E	L	I	F	E	O	F	G	R	A	C	E	A	C
A	G	S	B	U	W	O	M	H	J	U	A	U	S	V
T	S	L	R	S	O	U	L	O	H	K	X	E	L	L
N	J	T	G	I	F	T	Q	E	F	P	M	Y	S	V
L	I	E	G	B	I	M	A	G	E	J	I	N	T	E
K	N	O	W	I	N	G	G	O	D	A	S	X	H	P

Fill in the blanks.

God - soul - know - living - image - Grace

God created us in his own _____ and likeness. He created us body and _____, giving us a special kind of life called the life of _____. We are able to _____ and love God.

Grace is God _____ in our souls. It helps us to live as children of _____.

What I have learned

- People have a very important place in creation.
- God created us in his own image and likeness.
- God created us to have a body and a soul.
- Grace is God's presence in our souls. It helps us to live as children of God.

What I will always remember

Who are the most important parts of creation?
Man and woman are the most important parts of creation.

In what way did God create us?
God created us with bodies and souls, and in his own image and likeness.

What can we do that the rest of creation can't do?
We can know and love God.

What is "Grace"?
Grace is God's presence in our souls, which helps us to live as children of God.

What I am going to do

- I'm going to go to the chapel to ask God always to help me be very close to him and to live as his child.
- I'm going to invite a friend to go with me to do the same.

The Sacraments: Food for Our Souls

Jesus gave us a way to make the life of grace grow and become stronger and stronger in our souls. Because of this, God will always be in our hearts, and Jesus himself will always be our best friend.

This great gift is the gift we must give to everyone.

Today we're going to learn how the life of grace grows in our souls.

When Jesus went up to heaven

Just before returning to his Father in heaven on **Ascension** Day to be with his Father; Jesus told his apostles to bring his word to people everywhere.

He also gave them added encouragement for this task, promising them:

"I will be with you always, even to the end of the world."

These words made the apostles very happy because they knew Jesus would always be with them, even if they couldn't see him.

In the space provided, write what Jesus promised his apostles:

During his life on earth, Jesus gave us special ways, called sacraments, to keep this promise. Through the sacraments, he gives us his grace and helps us to keep God in our hearts, and get to heaven.

Our spiritual food

When you eat fruit and vegetables you grow big and healthy. You will have the strength you need to play, study, and always be joyful.

In the same way, you need to feed your soul so that the life of grace can grow healthy and strong in your soul.

The sacraments are the way Jesus chose

The sacraments are a great gift from Jesus Christ.
He instituted them to give us his grace so we can always have God in our hearts.

What are the sacraments?

Fill in the blanks using the symbols to help you.

The _____ are visible signs instituted by _____ and entrusted to the _____ to give us divine _____ and to help us reach heaven.

Life   **Church**   **Christ**   **Sacraments**

What do all these things mean?

Color the drawings.

Visible signs

The sacraments are made up of acts, things, and words that we can hear, see, and touch. In baptism, for example, there are the water and the words the priest says. Both of these signs stand for and bring about God's invisible action.

Made by Christ

Christ himself was the one who gave us the sacraments. He made them at different moments throughout his life. It is Christ himself who acts in each sacrament.

Entrusted to the Church

Christ commanded his apostles and their successors to celebrate the sacraments and bring them to all people.

To give us divine life

The sacraments are the food God gives us to nourish the special kind of life he has given us, the life of grace.

To achieve our salvation

If we nourish our souls properly, we will reach heaven.

How many sacraments are there, and what are their names?

There are seven sacraments

The first three are Baptism, Confirmation and the Eucharist; we call them the Sacraments of Initiation. Through these sacraments we become full members of God's family.

Baptism: Christ made this sacrament to wash us clean of original sin. Its unique graces make us children of God and members of his Church.

Confirmation: Through this sacrament we receive the Holy Spirit and all his gifts. We receive strength and help to live out our faith; Confirmation unites us more deeply to Christ and his Church.

The Eucharist: This is the sacrament of Christ's Body and Blood under the appearances of bread and wine. Since this is Christ himself, the Eucharist is the sum and source of the remaining Sacraments.

Reconcilation and Penance (or Confession): This is the sacrament Christ instituted to forgive sins committed after baptism.

Matrimony: Through this sacrament God blesses the union of a man and a woman within the Church.

Holy Orders: This sacrament gives a man a special participation in the priesthood of Christ and special graces for the good of the Church.

Anointing of the Sick: This sacrament gives special grace and strength to those who are elderly or sick, helping them to accept their condition. It gives strength to the body and the soul.

Complete the crossword puzzle on the sacraments.

1 across: Gives special grace to the elderly and sick.

2 down: God blesses the union of a man and a woman.

3 down: We receive the Holy Spirit and all his gifts.

4 across: Gives man a special participation in Christ's priesthood, making him "another Christ."

5 across: Grants forgiveness for sins committed after baptism.

6 down: Christ's own Body and Blood under the appearances of bread and wine.

7 across: Wipes away original sin and makes us children of God.

What I have learned

- Jesus wished to stay with us and give us his grace through the sacraments.
- The sacraments are food for our spiritual lives.
- Jesus himself instituted the sacraments and entrusted them to the Church.

What I will always remember

What are the sacraments?
The sacraments are visible signs instituted by Christ and entrusted to the Church for our salvation and for the growth of the divine life within us.

How many sacraments are there, and what are their names?
There are seven sacraments: Baptism, Confirmation, the Eucharist, Penance and Reconciliation (Confession), Anointing of the Sick, Holy Orders, and Matrimony.

What I am going to do

- I'm going to make a real effort to be a worthy child of God, keeping the life of grace alive in my soul.
- Every night I'm going to ask Jesus to help all my friends be very close to him.

The Holy Spirit Provides Strength and Comfort

When Jesus told us to go out into the whole world and preach the Gospel, we didn't think we'd be able to do it. Where would we get that kind of courage? What would we tell people? How would we have to act? We thought we'd never be able to do it. That's why Jesus promised to send us the Holy Spirit: to help us and to give us courage and strength.

Today we're going to learn how the Holy Spirit helps us and gives us the strength we need.

The day of Pentecost

On the feast of Pentecost all of us apostles got together to pray. Jesus' mother, the Virgin Mary, was also with us. We remembered Jesus told us, before he went to heaven, that he would send us his Spirit.

Suddenly we heard a loud noise and saw tongues of fire that rested on our heads.

These tongues of fire were the Holy Spirit coming to give us the help and strength we would need to do what Jesus had commanded.

The Spirit showed himself as the Spirit of communion, who abides indefectibly in the Church. The most intimate cooperation between the two is achieved in the Liturgy where the Holy Spirit is sent in order to bring us into communion with Christ and so to form his body.

Now we could carry out our mission!

Now that you've read about what happened on the day of Pentecost, fill in the blanks below.

The _____ and the Virgin Mary were gathered
together on the day of _____. While together,
_____ of fire came down and rested on their heads.
These tongues of fire are the _____ _____ who would
help them and give them the _____ they needed to
carry out their mission.

Before and After

Before Pentecost, the apostles were very afraid. They didn't know how they could carry out the mission Jesus had given them. They hid themselves because they were afraid. They needed special strength.

After Pentecost, the apostles had the help and the strength of the Holy Spirit to carry out their mission.

The Holy Spirit helps us, too. With his help we can
- understand what Jesus wants to teach us.
- live as true children of God.
- do what God asks of us.
- love one another as true brothers and sisters.
- be kind and loving towards one and all.

The Holy Spirit is at work in each of the sacraments. He makes us all come together with each other and with Christ, and gives us the help and strength we need to live as Christ has taught us and reach heaven.

Color these children being helped by the Holy Spirit.

Steve knows it's very important to know Jesus and so he pays close attention in religion class. The Holy Spirit helps him to understand what his teacher says.

All the second-grade students know that they should treat each other as true brothers and sisters, and the Holy Spirit helps them too.

Elizabeth and Tom know that to be good sons and daughters of God they must be very obedient. The Holy Spirit helps them obey their parents.

Ann knows that to be like Jesus she needs to help others and love them. The Holy Spirit gives her the strength to help her classmates.

Trust in the Holy Spirit. He will always help you and give you the strength you need to live as a good son or daughter of God.

Draw several children walking along this road, reaching their final goal with the help of the Holy Spirit.

How can the Holy Spirirt help you?

Respond below.

The Holy Spirit is your great friend and always wants to help you.

Say this prayer every day:

Prayer to the Holy Spirit.

Come, Holy Spirit, fill the hearts of your faithful
and kindle in them the fire of your love.

Send forth your Spirit and they shall be created,
and you will renew the face of the earth.

Lord, by the light of the Holy Spirit
you have taught the hearts of your faithful.
In the same Spirit help us to relish what is right
and always rejoice in your consolation.
We ask this through Christ Our Lord.
Amen.

Match the sentences on the left with the words on the right by putting the correct number in each box.

1. The apostles were gathered together with Mary on the day of
2. After Pentecost, the apostles
3. Gives us the strength to live as true children of God:
4. The Holy Spirit is at work in each one of the
5. The Holy Spirit came down on the apostles in the form of

☐ tongues of fire.

☐ The Holy Spirit.

☐ had the strength they needed to carry out their mission.

☐ the Sacraments.

☐ Pentecost.

What I have learned

- The Holy Spirit came to the apostles and Mary on the day of Pentecost.
- The Holy Spirit is at work in the sacraments.
- The Holy Spirit helps us to understand what Jesus teaches us.
- The Holy Spirit gives us the strength we need to live as true children of God.
- The Holy Spirit deepens our love for one another, enabling us to live as brothers and sisters.
- We should trust in the Holy Spirit and ask him to help us.

What I will always remember

What happened on the day of Pentecost?
Jesus sent the Holy Spirit down to Mary and the apostles.

Who is the Holy Spirit?
The Holy Spirit is the Third Person of the Holy Trinity.

Where is the Holy Spirit at work?
The Holy Spirit is at work in the sacraments.

What I am going to do

- I'm going to say my prayers every morning, offering my day to God and asking the Holy Spirit to help me live as a good Christian.

38

thirty-eight

Baptism: A New Life

When you were all very small, your parents and godparents took you to church to receive the first of all the sacraments.

Have any of you ever been to a baptism?

Some of us apostles were there when Jesus was baptized.

Today we're going to learn how we have been born into a new life.

One day at the Jordan River

One day, John the Baptist was at the Jordan River. People were coming to him from all over to be baptized.
Jesus came too, and asked John to baptize him.
When John saw Jesus, he said, "You are coming to me to be baptized? I'm the one who needs to be baptized by you!"
Jesus answered: "Baptize me. We must do as God wishes."

So John baptized Jesus.
The sky opened up and the Holy Spirit came down in the form of a dove and rested on Jesus' head. God's voice could be heard saying, "This is my beloved Son..."

This is how Jesus teaches us the importance of the sacrament of Baptism.

Color the drawing and fill in the missing words.

"You come to be _____ by me?
I am the one who needs to be baptized by you!"

"This is my beloved ____..."

What is the Sacrament of Baptism?

Baptism is the first sacrament we receive.
To be able to receive the rest of the sacraments we must first receive the sacrament of Baptism.

Through Baptism Adam and Eve's original sin, which we are all born with, is washed away from our souls.

It is the sacrament that gives us the great gift of the life of grace because it brings God into our souls.

Baptism makes us sons and daughters of God and gives us membership in his Church as the People of God.

Through Baptism we are born into a new life in Christ.

How do we get baptized?

Finish the drawings by writing on the lines provided in what the priest and parents say.

When a baby is born the parents are very happy and so are the godparents. Together, they take the child to church. The priest welcomes them and asks them, "What do you want for this child?" They answer that they want the great gift of faith for the child.

After that, the priest pours some water over the child's head, saying his or her name and the words,

"I baptize you in the name of the Father, and of the Son, and of the Holy Spirit."

At that moment the child receives the new life of grace. God enters the child's heart, and everyone is very happy.

The priest also hands a lighted candle to the godparents, and everyone prays the Our Father together.

Jesus himself instituted the sacrament of Baptism

Color these drawings. Study them carefully and in the space below write what they represent.

_____
_____
_____
_____
_____
_____
_____

Which words are the same in the two pictures? Write them down here:

_____
_____

In each box write the number of the object that goes with the sentence.

☐ It is the sign that we can see. When the priest pours it, the child's soul is washed clean.

☐ Stands for the light we get from being sons and daughters of God.

☐ The one who baptizes the child, standing in for Jesus.

☐ The ones who are to take care of the life of faith of the child in the event that the parents are unable to do so.

☐ Are very happy because their child is now a child of God!

☐ A new member of the Church.

Fill in the blanks.

original sin - baptism - Church - God - sacrament - souls - Christ

Through the sacrament of _____ we are born into a new life in _____ .

Baptism is the first _____ we receive.

Through baptism _____ _____ is washed from our souls and we receive God into our _____ .

Through this sacrament we become children of _____ and members of his great family, the _____ .

What I have learned

- John the Baptist baptized Jesus in the Jordan River.
- Jesus gave his apostles the mission of baptizing all people in the name of the Father, the Son, and the Holy Spirit.
- In baptism we are born into a new life in Christ.
- Baptism is the first sacrament we receive.
- Through baptism, original sin is washed from our souls; God enters our souls; we become sons and daughters of God; and we begin to form part of his family, the Church.

What I will always remember

What is the sacrament of Baptism?

It is the sacrament Jesus Christ instituted to wash away original sin, and to make us children of God and members of the Church.

What is the first sacrament we receive?

The first sacrament we receive is Baptism, since without it we cannot receive the rest of the sacraments.

When did Christ institute the sacrament of Baptism?

When he said to his apostles, "Go and make disciples of all peoples, baptizing them in the name of the Father, the Son, and the Holy Spirit."

What I am going to do

- Every night before going to bed I'm going to thank God for making me his own child through Baptism. I'm going to ask him to help me be a good Christian.

We Are Children of God

Every day, Jesus would leave us apostles on our own for a little while. Do you know why? Jesus would go off and pray. He talked to God, his Father, every day. One day we asked him to teach us pray. That's when he taught us the prayer you already know, the Our Father.

Today we're going to learn that we can call God "our Father".

Jesus always talked to his Father

Color these drawings.

Jesus prayed every day.

One day the apostles asked him to teach them to pray.

Jesus taught them the Our Father. From that moment on, the apostles called God their Father.

You and your friends also pray to God, our Father.

Through Baptism we became children of God. Thanks to our baptism we can call God "Father."

God is our Father

At the time of their baptism infants aren't able to talk yet. That's why the parents and godparents and everyone present prays the Our Father together, calling God our "Father."

Draw an infant being baptized with the other people there praying the Our Father.

Fill in the blanks.

baptism - God - loves - Father - children

God is our_____ who gives us life and _____us. Through _____ God gives us new life and makes us his_____.

Thanks to baptism , we can call _____ our Father.

We are children of God

We have a Father who is very good to us and loves us very much. We should be good sons and daughters and love him very much.

To be good sons and daughters of God we should

love him.

**How can you show God you love him very much?
Write your answer below:**

At home:_____

_____

At school:_____

_____

praise him.

**Praying every day is a way to praise God.
Write a short prayer to God, your Father.**

_____

_____

_____

_____

thank him.

**What do you have tohat you can thank God for?
Prepare a list below.**

_____

_____

_____

_____

ask him for whatever we need with great trust.

Go to your school chapel and pray to God, your Father, for all the people you love, for the needs of people everywhere, and for peace in the world.

Heaven is our inheritance

God has a great gift in store for all his sons and daughters.

Heaven is a state of total joy in which we will be united to God. God wants all of us to reach heaven. He helps us with his Grace so we can get there and be happy with God, our Father.

Draw very happy faces on these children and then color them. Color the phrase below, too.

We are very happy because we are children of God and are invited to heaven.

In the alphabet soup below find the words that are missing from these sentences.

Jesus taught his apostles the Our _____.

Through _____we become children of _____.

God is our Father who gives us his _____and loves us.

To be good children of God we should _____ him, praise him,_____ him, and ask him to help us in our needs.

God wants all his children to reach _____.

In heaven we will be _____ once and for all to God, our Father.

```
L O P Y F R J K L M H A P P Y S O L A
F A T H E R O U R L M Y R D J I T
P L Q A Z X P K J G A M A R L O V E I Y
I D G O D L G A L U N I T E D I Y U K E O
E P K J V I D A O F A T H A R G R A C E I R
H E A V E N L R A V V H R K I L D I D I W I
O T R S D O E J K I B A P T I S M N L W
O L T H A N K S L O K N O K H T I F E
```

What I have learned

- Jesus taught us the Our Father.
- Through Baptism we become children of God. We can call God our Father.
- To be good sons and daughters of God we should love him, praise him, thank him, and ask him to help us in all our needs.
- God wants all his children to be with him in heaven.

What I will always remember

What prayer did Jesus teach us?
He taught us the Our Father.

What has God invited his children to?
To be with him in heaven.

What I am going to do

- I'm going to show God how much I love him by striving to be a good son or daughter of his, both at home and at school.
- I'm going to pray to God every night for all the people that are far away from him.

Overcoming Temptation

When we apostles were living with Jesus, we always wanted to be near him, close by to hear everything he was saying, and to be his friends.

All of you want to be good sons and daughters of God, too. You all want to be Jesus' friends, right?

So why is it sometimes hard to live exactly as he wants us to live?

Today we're going to learn how to overcome temptations in order to always be united to Jesus.

One day in the desert

After Jesus was baptized by John the Baptist, he went off into the desert and stayed there for forty days. He wanted to be alone to pray, to be very close to God, and to get ready to preach the Gospel and save us from sin.

When the forty days were over, the devil came to Jesus to try to make him sin. He tried to tempt him.

Jesus didn't pay any attention to the temptations the devil put before him, and so the devil left him.

The devil had been a very beautiful and intelligent angel. But he wanted to be more important than God and more intelligent than him. He rebelled against God and separated himself from him forever.

The devil can never return to heaven to be with God, and he doesn't want us to get to heaven either. He puts things in our way to keep us from getting there.

He tries to make us do evil by putting temptations on our path.

Look at the road leading to the top of the mountain. Draw a circle around all the things the children have to overcome to remain on the road and reach their goal. These things are temptations.

We're not alone when we're tempted

The sacrament of Baptism gives us the strength we need to say "No" to the temptations the devil places before us. Baptism guarantees us the help of God's grace and his friendship.

At Baptism, the parents and godparents of the child make promises on his or her behalf, promising always to stay close to God and to say no to the devil and his temptations.

Color this drawing and what it represents on the lines below.

We, too, can overcome temptation

In the space provided write what you need to do in each situation in order to overcome any possible temptations.

It's 7:00 p.m. Your mother tells you it's time to take a bath and get ready for bed.
What should you do?

_____
_____
_____
_____
_____

Your siblings ask you to lend them one of your toys and play with them.
What should you do?

_____
_____
_____
_____
_____

It's time to do your homework, but there's a TV show that you really want to watch.
What should you do?

_____
_____
_____
_____

You're in math class and you need to pay attention to learn to divide.
What should you do?

_____
_____
_____
_____

You were planning to play with a friend, but another friend has asked you to help her with something.
What should you do?

_____
_____
_____
_____

There are many ways to overcome temptation

Fill in the blanks using the words with colored dots that match the colors of the lines.

I can overcome temptation by...

• _____ to God for help.
• Listening to what God tells me through my _____, my _____, and my _____.
• Following my _____, which helps me to know what is pleasing to God and what takes me away from him.
It helps me to overcome_____ and stay close to _____.

⬤ priest ⬤ temptation ⬤ teachers ⬤ Praying

⬤ parents ⬤ God ⬤ conscience

Write in the part that's missing from the Our Father and you'll see how every time you pray it you're asking God to help you overcome temptation.

Our Father, who art in heaven, hallowed be thy name.
Thy kingdom come, thy will be done,
on earth as it is in heaven.
Give us this day our daily bread and
forgive us our trespasses
as we forgive those who trespass against us.
and lead us not into

_____,
but deliver us from evil.
Amen.

Match the sentences on the left with the words on the right by writing the correct number in each box.

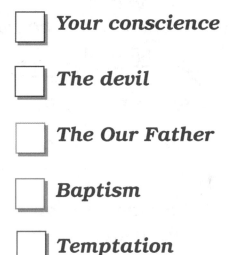

1. He was a beautiful angel who rebelled against God.

2. What the devil puts before us to take us away from God.

3. In this sacrament we promise to overcome temptation.

4. Helps you to do what is right and know what is pleasing to God.

5. Praying this every day will help you overcome temptation.

☐ **Your conscience**

☐ **The devil**

☐ **The Our Father**

☐ **Baptism**

☐ **Temptation**

What I have learned

- Temptation is what the devil places on our path to try to get us to do evil.
- Jesus overcame the temptations the devil put before him in the desert.
- We, too, can overcome temptation with the help of God's Grace.
- At Baptism we promise to overcome temptation.
- My conscience helps me to know what is right and overcome temptation.
- When I pray the Our Father I ask God to help me overcome temptation.

What I will always remember

What is temptation?

It is what the devil places on our path to get us to do evil.

Can we overcome temptation?

Yes, with the help of God's grace.

What do we mean by "conscience?"

Conscience is the voice of God in our souls helping us always to live as friends of Christ, doing what is right and overcoming temptation.

What I am going to do

- I'm going to go to the chapel and ask God to help me keep the promise I made at Baptism never to give in to temptation.
- I'm going to ask a friend to go with me to the chapel to pray an Our Father.
- When I feel like doing something wrong, I'm going to ask my conscience how I should behave. I'm also going to remember that God's Grace will help me overcome the temptation and stay close to Jesus.

One Big Family

When we apostles were with Jesus, he explained that he wanted to start a big family and leave one of us in charge of watching over it and taking care of it.

All of you belong to this big family started by Jesus. Do you know what it is called?

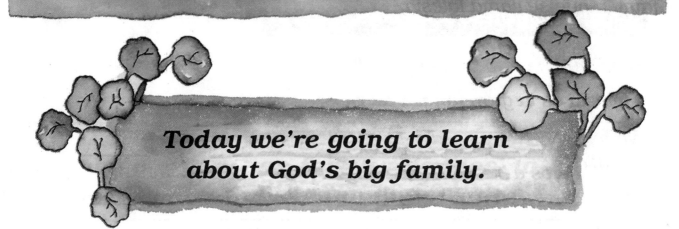

Today we're going to learn about God's big family.

Jesus said to Peter

One day, Jesus said to Peter

"You are Peter, which means 'rock,' and on this rock I will build my Church."

Another time Jesus said to him:
"Peter, feed my lambs."

Jesus also promised Peter and the rest of his apostles that he would never leave them on their own.

Peter became the first one to be in charge of the Church, which is God's big family.

One big family

When you were baptized, God invited you to belong to his great and big family, which is the Church.

Copy down these sentences.

The Church is God's great family.

_____

_____

We became part of God's family, the Church, when we were baptized.

_____

_____

In a family, everyone is important

Every member of the Church is very important. We are all brothers and sisters to Christ and one another. We are all children of God. When someone in the family is sick or is having problems, everyone gets worried.

Draw lines connecting the family members on the left with what they do on the right.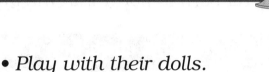

Dad

Mom

Brothers

Sisters

Grandparents

Aunts and Uncles

- • Play with their dolls.

- • Loves us and takes care of us. She cooks and looks after us.

- • Love us very much, and we go to visit them.

- • Loves us and takes care of us. He works so that we have everything we need.

- • Love us very much and come to visit us, bringing their children, our cousins, with them.

- • Play with toy cars.

In God's Great Family, the Church, all of us are very important, too!

In the Church, we are all very important

Take a careful look at this drawing. It is a church being built out of bricks, with windows, doors, and a roof.
Every brick must be strong or the church will start to fall apart or possibly collapse.

The Church is made up of each one of us, and we need to be good Catholics so it will be strong and never collapse.
We are all very important in the great family of the Church.

Write a name on each brick. You may write your own name, the names of friends, your parents, your brothers and sisters, your relatives, your priest, etc.

Every part of the body is important

This is Paul.
He's on the school soccer team.
He's a very good soccer player.
He's in good shape and eats everything his mother serves him.

A few days ago something happened.
Paul went running through the doorway to his house and stubbed his toe.

Do you think he'll be able to play soccer as well as he usually plays, even though the rest of his body is in great shape?

Circle the correct answer.

 YES   **NO**

Why?_____

_____

In the church building

In Pauls body

the bricks are for

_____

_____

his eyes are for

_____

_____

the windows are for

_____

_____

his legs are for

_____

_____

the doors are for

_____

_____

his hands are for

_____

_____

We all have a part to play

In the Church, too, we all have an important role that we must fulfill so that the whole church will be healthy and strong.

What role do teachers have?_____
_____

What role do parents have?_____
_____

What role do priests have?_____
_____

What role do boys and girls like you have?_____
_____

Every one of us should perform our duty out of love for God. With our support the Church will always be healthy and strong.

God's Great Family, the Church, has shepherds who watch over it and take care of it.

Jesus chose to place Peter and the apostles in charge of taking care of his Church. Peter became the first pope.

There is someone who is in charge of the Church, too. He is the pope. Just as the apostles helped Peter, today's bishops and priests help the pope guide the Church. They teach us the Faith, help us to be holy and very close to God, and show us the way to heaven.

Glue a picture of the Pope here, and write his name in the blank below.

Pope _____ is the leader
of the Church. God has given him the job of taking care of us,
just as he gave the same job to Peter.

What is the Church that Jesus started like?

Here are the **characteristic marks** of the Church Jesus started:

It is One
This is because the Church was started by one man, Jesus; because it has only one doctrine, the one Jesus taught; and because it has only one main leader on earth, the pope.

It is Holy
This is because Jesus makes the Church holy by always being with it in the sacraments. It is also holy because the Holy Spirit helps all of us as members of the Church to be holy.

It is Catholic
The Church is "catholic," or "universal," because it is God's family made up of people from all over the world, people of every race, culture, and society.

It is Apostolic
This is because it is the same Church that Jesus started with his apostles. It is also apostolic because it teaches us the same doctrine that Jesus taught his apostles and because the Church's bishops have taken the place of the first apostles.

Complete the phrases on the left with the correct phrases on the right by coloring the church the color of the number in front of the matching phrase.

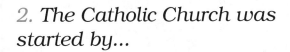

1. God's great family is called...

very important.

2. The Catholic Church was started by...

it is meant for everybody, no matter who they are.

3. The Church's first Pope and leader, was...

the pope, the bishops, and priests.

4. In God's great family, we are all...

Christ started it with his apostles.

5. These are our good shepherds...

the Church.

6. The Church is One because...

Christ makes it Holy.

7. The Church is Holy because...

Jesus Christ.

8. The Church is Catholic because...

it has only one founder (one person who started it), and only one doctrine, or teaching.

9. The Church is Apostolic because...

St. Peter.

What I have learned

- The Church is God's great family.
- Jesus Christ started, or founded, the Church.
- St. Peter was chosen to be the first leader of the Church.
- We belong to the Church from the day of our baptism.
- In the Church, every member is very important.
- We have our own good shepherds in the Church: the pope, the bishops, and priests.
- The Church Christ founded is One, Holy, Catholic, and Apostolic.

What I will always remember

What is the Church?
It is God's great family, to which every baptized Catholic belongs.

Who founded, or started, the Catholic Church?
Jesus Christ founded the Catholic Church.

What are the characteristic marks of the Church Jesus founded?
It is One, Holy, Catholic, and Apostolic.

What I am going to do

- I'm going to strive every day to be a good member of the Church by being an obedient child and a hard-working student.

The Commandments:
Our Road to Heaven

Jesus taught us many things to reach heaven.
But even before that, God gave us some rules for getting to heaven. Do all of you know what you have to do to reach heaven?

Today we're going to learn about the road map God has given us to reach heaven.

On the way to the Promised Land

The Israelites, the first Jews, were God's chosen people. At one point they turned away from God and became slaves in Egypt for many years.

God had pity on them and wanted to save them from their slavery. He chose a man named Moses to free them from their slavery in Egypt and lead them to a land of their own, the Promised Land. As he led them away from Egypt and towards the Promised Land, Moses stopped to climb Mt. Sinai to speak with God.

It was then that God entrusted to Moses a great gift, two stone tablets that had written on them what we all must do to reach heaven. These laws are difficult, but God gives us the graces we need to obey them.

**On Mt. Sinai Moses received from God
the tablets containing the Ten Commandments.**

Fill in the blanks.

guide - Sinai - Israelites - heaven - tablets - Moses
Egypt - Promised - Commandments

The _____ lived as slaves in _____.
God called _____ to free the Israelites and lead them to
the _____ Land.

On his way there, Moses climbed Mt. _____ and received
from God two stone _____ containing the
Ten _____.
The Ten Commandments are our sure _____ for
reaching _____.

The Ten Commandments

Use the numbers to find the correct words and fill in the blanks, completing the Ten Commandments. Color the tablets once you have filled in the blanks.

I. You shall 1._____ the Lord your 2._____ above all things.

II. You shall not take the Name of the Lord your God in 3._____ .

III. You shall keep the Lord's day 4._____ .

1. Love
2. God
3. vain
4. holy
5. Honor

6. father
7. mother
8. kill
9. commit
10. steal

11. lie
12. thoughts
13. goods
14. things
15. neighbor

IV.5._____ your
6._____ and your 7._____ .

V. You shall not 8._____ .

VI. You shall not 9._____
      acts of impurity.

VII. You shall not 10._____.

VII. You shall not 11._____
      or give false witness.

IX. You shall not consent to
impure 12._____ or desires.

X. You shall not covet your
neighbor's 13._____ .

These Ten Commandments can
   be summed up in two
commandments: To love God
above all 14._____ and
to love one's 15._____
      as oneself.

What I have learned

- God gave Moses the Ten Commandments on Mt. Sinai.
- The commandments are a gift from God to help us reach heaven.
- To reach heaven we must keep the commandments.

What I will always remember

What are the Ten Commandments?
They are a gift from God to help us reach heaven.

Name the Ten Commandments.
The Ten Commandments are:
1. You shall love the Lord your God above all things.
2. You shall not take the name of the Lord your God in vain.
3. You shall keep the Lord's day holy.
4. You shall honor your father and your mother.
5. You shall not kill.
6. You shall not commit impure acts.
7. You shall not steal.
8. You shall not lie or give false witness.
9. You shall not consent to impure thoughts or desires.
10. You shall not covet your neighbor's goods.

What I am going to do

- I'm going to pay very close attention in religion class so that I can learn how to reach heaven.
- I'm going to help my friends pay close attention in religion class, too.

The Commandments: God and Me

Of course, you remember that God is our Father, gave us life, and loves us.

But did you know there's a way we can live up to this great love God has for us?

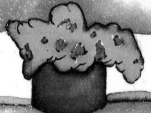

Today we're going to find out how we can show God we love him.

What is the first commandment?

Once when Jesus was teaching the people, a very wise man came up to him. The man was an expert in God's law. He said to Jesus: "Master, which commandment is the greatest?"

Jesus answered: "You shall love the Lord your God with all your heart, with all your soul, and with all your strength. This is the first and greatest Commandment."

On that day, Jesus reminded us of the first and most important commandment.

Fill in the blanks.

The First Three Commandments

The first three commandments teach us how we should behave towards God.

Do you remember what they are?

Write them down here.

1._____

2._____

3._____

These three commandments teach us how we should behave towards God, our Father and Creator. They show us how we can live up to God's immense love for us. He has made us his children!

The First Commandment
You shall love God above all else.

The first commandment instructs us to believe, trust, and love God more than anything or anyone else.

To live according to this Commandment

- **God must have the most important place in my life**
- **I'm always going to believe in God, my Father, who gave me my life and loves me**
- **I'm also going to trust in God. He is my Father and loves me very much**
- **I'm going to love God more than I love anything else. I need to give him the most important place in my life**

Complete the story, drawing in the empty box.

What can this boy do to keep the First Commandment?

Augustine's alarm clock goes off every morning,

and he gets out of bed.

Then Augustine offers the day to God.

Monica is having lots of fun with her friends.

She remembers that God has given her many things.

Monica gives thanks to God.

John hears the bell for the end of the class.

He passes the church on his way home.

John goes in to say hello to Jesus.

To see if I am keeping the first commandment, I'm going to ask myself:

Is God more important to me than anything else?

Do I tell God that I love him?

Do I thank him for all that he has given me?

Do I do it every day?

The Second Commandment
You shall not take the name of the Lord your God in vain.

The second commandment instructs us to respect God's name and to respect all sacred objects.

In order to keep this commandment
I'm going to use God's name with great love and respect.
I also need to respect and take good care of anything related to God.
Finally, I need to respect my priest and anyone devoted to serving God.

Color only those drawings that show children who are keeping the second Commandment.

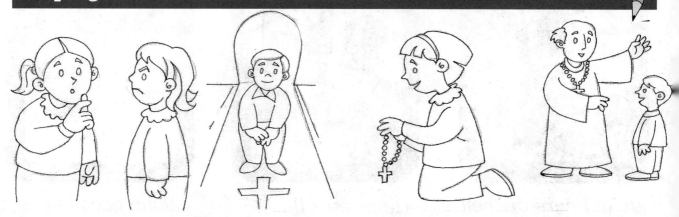

To see if I am keeping the second commandment, I'm going to ask myself:

Do I use God's name with devotion and respect, never using his name to swear?

Do I show special respect for things related to God, things such as the chapel, my Bible, and my rosary?

Do I show respect for priests and people devoted to serving God?

The Third Commandment
Keep the Lord's day holy.

The third commandment instructs us to dedicate Sundays and holy days to praising God and enjoying wholesome rest.

To keep this commandment

I need to go to Mass every Sunday and on the holy days the Church indicates. At Mass I should celebrate God's great love and all that he has done for us.
I should also use my Sundays to pray more than usual and to be very close to God, as well as take time to relax and help others relax and enjoy themselves.

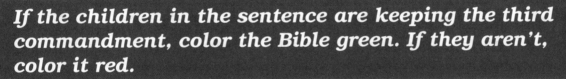

If the children in the sentence are keeping the third commandment, color the Bible green. If they aren't, color it red.

- Jane and Steve go to church every Sunday and pay close attention.

- Mary tries to pay close attention at Mass and be very close to God.

- Jim and Dan were very tired, so they decided to sleep instead of going to church.

- Tony had a football game today, so he didn't go to church.

- Charlie and Ann realized they wouldn't be able to go to church on Sunday, so they went on Saturday afternoon.

To see if I'm keeping the third commandment, I'm going to ask myself:

Do I go to church every Sunday and on the other days I should?

Do I try to be very close to God during Mass and listen to what he might be saying to me?

Do I think about God on Sundays?

Do I help others relax and enjoy themselves?

What I have learned

- We show God that we love him by keeping the commandments.
- The first three commandments teach us how we should treat God, our Father and Creator.

What I will always remember

Can the Ten Commandments be summarized?
Yes, they can be summed up in the two following commandments: Love God above all else and your neighbor as yourself.

List the commandments that teach us how to treat God:
They are the first three commandments:
- You shall love the Lord your God above all else.
- You shall not take the name of the Lord your God in vain.
- You shall keep the Lord's day holy.

What I am going to do

- I'm going to show God that he has the most important place in my life, and I will offer him my daily work.
- When I go to a church, I will behave.

The Commandments: My Neighbor and Me

Jesus taught us to love others.

He always said that if we want to be his friends we have to love one another as we love ourselves.

Today we're going to learn how we are to love our neighbor.

Who is my neighbor?

When Jesus was asked who this neighbor is that we need to love as we love ourselves, he told his listeners the parable of the Good Samaritan.

A man was traveling by foot from one city to another when some thieves attacked him and left him lying wounded on the road. As he lay there, three different men came by at different times. One was a Pharisee, one was an expert in Jewish law, and the other was a Samaritan.

The Pharisee and the law expert avoided the wounded man when they saw him lying there, continuing on their way without helping him at all.

But the Samaritan stopped to help him. He even took him to a nearby inn where his wounds could be treated. The Samaritan paid for the wounded man's care and then continued on his journey.

Which of the three men loved his neighbor as himself?

Explain

_____

Number the pictures of the parable according to the order in which they happened.

The first three commandments tell us how we should love God.
The other seven tell us about our duties towards our neighbor, how we should love our brothers and sisters.

Everyone everywhere is my neighbor!

The Fourth Commandment
You shall honor your father and your mother.

The fourth commandment instructs us to honor and respect our parents. God has given them the authority to care for us and guide us.

To keep this commandment
I should listen to, respect, and love my parents, as well as those who look after me and teach me, such as my teachers, my grandparents, and priests.

Draw a happy face on the children if they are keeping the Fourth commandment. Draw a sad face if they are not.

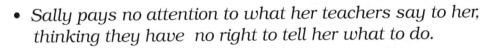

- Lucy and Joe always treat their grandparents with a lot of respect and affection.

- Mary always does what her parents tell her to do.

- Sally pays no attention to what her teachers say to her, thinking they have no right to tell her what to do.

- Johnny helps his parents out at home.

- Charlie hates it when he has to go along to visit his grandparents.

- Matthew knows that what his parents tell him is for his good.

- Paul pretends not to hear his parents when they tell him to do something.

To see if I'm keeping the fourth commandment, I'm going to ask myself

Do I obey my parents and everyone else who has authority over me?

Do I respect my parents and do what they ask of me, for my own good and safety?

Do I help my parents by doing the chores they give me? Do I show them love and thank them for everything they do for me?

The Fifth Commandment
You shall not kill.

The fifth commandment instructs us to respect our own life and that of our neighbor, taking care of our health. This is because human life is sacred.

To keep this commandment
I should treat others with love and respect, take care of myself, and be concerned about others.

If the picture shows a child keeping the fifth commandment, color the circle green. If the child is not keeping the Commandment, color the circle red.

To see if I'm keeping the fifth commandment, I'm going to ask myself.
Do I always treat others with kindness and respect: do I always try to say good things about them?
Do I always help others whenever I can?
Do I take care of myself, eating right to grow up healthy and strong, exercising, and practicing good hygiene?

The Sixth Commandment
You shall not commit impure acts.

The sixth commandment instructs us to keep our bodies and souls pure.

To keep this commandment
I believe that a pure body and soul are great treasures that I should always cherish and protect. My body is a temple of the Holy Spirit and so I should take very good care of it.

Color the bird green if the boy or girl is keeping the Sixth commandment. Color it red if he or she is not.

• *Mary cares for her body because she knows it's a gift from God*

• *Andy doesn't respect other people's privacy*

• *Lucy always closes her door when she gets changed*

• *James is very respectful towards the other boys and girls in his class*

To see if I am keeping the Sixth commandment, I'm going to ask myself:

Do I treat my body as a temple of the Holy Spirit?
Do I take care of my body, realizing that it is a great gift from God?
Do I respect my own privacy and that of others?

The Seventh Commandment
You shall not steal.

The seventh commandment instructs me to respect others' belongings, and to use my own belongings for my good and the good of others. It also instructs me to respect and take care of nature.

To keep this commandment

This commandment tells me that I shouldn't take anything that isn't mine, and that I shouldn't damage what belongs to others. It also teaches me to respect nature and to use things for good, and not for evil.

Finish the story by drawing children who follow the Seventh commandment.

Roger found something at his desk that didn't belong to him.

Sandra realized that there are other kids who don't have as much as she has.

To see if I am keeping the seventh commandment, I'm going to ask myself:

When I find things that aren't mine, do I return them?
Do I take care of the things I borrow from others?
Do I respect and take care of nature?
Do I share what I have with others who have less?

The Eighth Commandment
You shall not lie or give false witness.

The Eighth commandment instructs us to be honest and not to lie.

> **To live this commandment**
> I must be honest and never lie.
> It also tells me I must never deceive others or
> speak badly of them.

Draw a circle around those who are fulfilling the Eighth commandment.

To see if I'm keeping the eighth commandment I'm going to ask myself:

Am I always honest?
Do I handle bad situations without lying?
Do I say good things about others, or do I gossip about them?

The Ninth Commandment
You shall not consent to impure thoughts or desires.

The Ninth commandment tells us to keep our hearts pure so that we can see everything through God's eyes.

> **To live the commandment**
> I should watch over the
> purity of my heart, staying away from anything
> that can stain it.

Color the tablets of the law green if the boy or girl is keeping the ninth commandment. Color the tablets red if he or she is not.

- *Betty never wishes evil on anyone.*

- *Frank is a good friend to everybody.*

- *Johnny watches TV shows that he shouldn't.*

- *Peter realizes there are games and jokes that stain the purity of his heart so he refuses to play them or listen to them.*

- *Patty refuses to forgive others, bearing grudges in her heart for a long time.*

To see if I am keeping the ninth commandment I'm going to ask myself:

Do I have good thoughts towards everyone around me?
Do I try to make sure there are only good thoughts and feelings in my heart?
Do I avoid games and other things that stain my heart?
Do I make sure not to watch or hear anything on TV that could stain my soul?

The Tenth Commandment
You shall not covet your neighbor's goods.

The Tenth commandment instructs us to be generous-hearted and not to let envy enter our hearts.

> **To keep this commandment**
> *I should be happy with what I've got and should not be envious of those who have more. It also tells me I must work for the things I want.*

Draw a happy face on those who are keeping the tenth commandment, and a sad face on those who aren't.

- *Bill spends Saturday mornings working around the house to earn money to buy a new bike.*

- *Judy is happy when a friend of hers gets something she wanted.*

- *Tony is upset because Luke has more toys than he has.*

- *Getting more than others is the only thing Ann thinks about.*

- *Johnny realizes there are other kids who have a lot less than he has so he shares his toys and play things with them.*

To see if I am fulfilling the tenth commandment I'm going to ask myself:

Am I happy with what I have?
Do I take care of and show gratitude for the things God has given me?
Do I feel happy when my friends get something I don't have?
Am I happy when things go well for others?

What I have learned

- To love God we must also love our neighbor.
- Everyone is my neighbor.
- The last seven commandments teach us how to treat our neighbor.

What I will always remember

Which commandments teach us how we should treat our neighbor?

The Fourth: You shall honor your father and your mother.
The Fifth: You shall not kill.
The Sixth: You shall not commit impure acts.
The Seventh: You shall not steal.
The Eighth: You shall not lie or give false witness.
The Ninth: You shall not consent to impure thoughts or desires.
The Tenth: You shall not covet your neighbor's goods.

What I am going to do
- I am going to go to the chapel to think sincerely about whether or not I love my neighbor as God requests, fulfilling the commandments.
- I am going to be a good friend towards all my classmates, treating them as if they were my own brothers and sisters.

The Precepts of the Church

When Jesus left us apostles in charge of his Church, he gave us the mission of helping all people reach heaven by passing on to them everything he taught us.

This is how the Church helps you reach heaven.

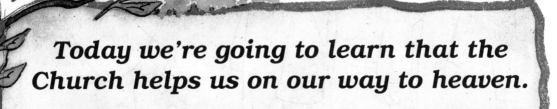

Today we're going to learn that the Church helps us on our way to heaven.

When Jesus founded the Church, he gave his apostles the strength and guidance to lead it.

He told them:
"**What you bind on earth shall be bound in heaven.
What you loose on earth shall be loosed in heaven.**"

Fill in the blanks, completing what Jesus said to his apostles. Then color the picture.

What you bind on _____ shall be bound in _____.
What you loose on earth, shall be _____ in heaven.

Throughout her history the Church has shown people the way to heaven and has helped them get there, just like a true mother and loving teacher.

Since the Church is Jesus' representative on earth, we need to do whatever her asks of us.

To obey the Church is to obey Jesus.

The Church's commandments, or precepts, are a guide for Catholics. The Church gives them to us to help us fulfill God's law better.

Fill in the blanks to complete the Church's precepts, using the numbers to help you.

The Precepts of the Church

I: You shall attend 1._____ **on Sundays and holy days of** 2._____ .

II: You shall 3._____ **your serious** 4._____ **at least once a year.**

III: You shall receive 5._____ **at least as is** 6._____ .

IV: You shall keep 7._____ **the holy days of** 8._____ .

V: You shall observe the prescribed days of 9._____ **and abstinence.**

The Church also calls us to 10._____ **her in her** 11._____ .

1. Mass	5. Communion	9. fasting
2. obligation	6. Easter	10. help
3. confess	7. holy	11. needs
4. sins	8. obligation	

The 1st and 4th. Attending Mass on Sundays and holy days of obligation:

To keep this precept we must go to Mass and try to be as attentive as possible.

3rd. Receive communion during Easter:

This precept instructs us to receive Communion at least once during Easter, but you may receive Communion every single day of the year. It's the very best way to be close to Jesus and eventually reach heaven.

5th. Help the Church in its needs:

The Church has a lot of needs, both spiritual and material. You, too, can help by making sacrifices, praying, or putting something in the collection basket on Sunday.

2nd. Go to Confession at least once a year:

To keep this precept we must confess any serious sins at least once a year. This precept also tells us that we must go to Confession before receiving Communion if we have committed a mortal sin. It's a very good idea to get into the habit of going to Confession regularly because it will help you remain in the state of grace and to have the strength to struggle against temptations, imitating Christ.

4th. Keep the prescribed days of fasting and abstinence:

The Church asks us to sacrifice throughout the year, especially during Lent. This helps us to grow in our love for God and others.

Read the sentence and then circle the number of the precept that the boy or girl is fulfilling.

Laura goes to Mass every Sunday and pays very close attention. 1 2 4 3 5 *

Mary goes to church on Christmas day. 1 2 4 3 5 *

Tony goes to Confession often. 1 2 4 3 5 *

Frank always receives Communion on Easter Sunday. 1 2 4 3 5 *

Louis goes to Communion every day at school. 1 2 4 3 5

Peter makes a special sacrifice on Ash Wednesday. 1 2 4 3 5 *

Ann doesn't eat any candy on Good Friday. 1 2 4 3 5 *

Jim prays for the Pope and the Church every night. 1 2 4 3 5 *

Lucy saves part of her allowance to put it in the basket on Sundays. 1 2 4 3 5 *

Andy says a prayer for his priest. 1 2 4 3 5 *

Fill in the blanks below.

Christians - apostles - heaven - Jesus - precepts - earth - Church

- Jesus said to his _____: "What you bind on _____, shall be bound in heaven."
- The Church shows us the way to _____ and helps us to get there.
- We need to obey the _____ because She is Christ's representative on earth.
- By obeying what the Church says we obey _____.
- The Church's _____ are a guide for Catholics. They help us to live as good _____.

What I have learned

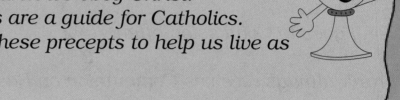

- Jesus has given his Church the task of showing us the way to heaven and helping us get there.
- When we obey the Church we obey Christ.
- The Church's precepts are a guide for Catholics.
- The Church gives us these precepts to help us live as good Christians.

What I will always remember

What are the precepts of the Church?
There are five precepts:
1: You shall attend Mass on Sundays and holy days of obligation.
2: You shall confess your serious sins at least once a year.
3: You shall receive Communion at least during Easter season.
4: You shall keep holy the holy days of obligation.
5: You shall observe the prescribed days of fasting and abstinence.
The Church also calls on us to help it in its needs.

What I am going to do

- I'm going to do my schoolwork well and offer it for the Church.
- I'm going to ask Jesus to help me always do what he tells me through the Church.

Our Friendship With Christ Is Lost Through Sin

For each of us apostles,
Jesus became our very best friend.
We didn't want to do anything that would hurt our friendship with
Jesus. So we always stayed close by his side, listening to everything
he told us and trying as hard as we could to put everything into
practice.

Today we're going to learn about the one and only thing that can destroy our friendship with Jesus.

A plant that produces lots of fruit.

Jesus once told us that each one of us should be like a healthy, productive grapevine, producing lots of grapes.

Grapevines have three parts.
First there's the grapevine itself.
Then, coming out of the vine, are the vinebranches.
Finally, at the end of the vinebranches, are the clusters of grapes.

Now think about this.
If the vinebranch is torn away from the vine...
will it be able to produce grapes?_____
Why not?_____
_____

Jesus wants to teach us something through this parable.

He is the vine and we are the branches.
Unless we are united to Jesus, unless we are in the state of
grace, we can't produce anything good.
In order for our actions to produce good results,
we must be united to Jesus.

What is the only thing that can tear us away from the vine?
What is the only thing that can separate us from Jesus?
Finish the word.

S___n.

**Sin is the only thing that can take us away from Jesus.
Sin kills the Life of Grace within us
and separates us from God.**

Mortal sin

It is called "mortal" because it kills our friendship with Christ. By seriously breaking God's law, we offend him and his love for us. Mortal sin sends God out of our hearts, killing the Life of Grace within us.

Venial sin

This kind of sin weakens our friendship with Jesus. It's a less serious offense, but it still keeps us from building a strong friendship with Christ. Venial sin can even lead us to commit mortal sin.

Write a brief letter to Jesus telling him that your friendship with him is the most important thing in your life and that you never want to hurt that friendship by sinning.

God is our Father. He loves us and created us to be happy, but we can't be happy if we are far away from him. That's why God wants us to stay close to him, never turning away from him by sinning.

Put a happy face on these children if their actions have brought them closer to God. Put a sad face on them if they have turned away from God by sinning.

- Edward knows he should always obey his parents, and he does so happily.

- Tony didn't do his homework as he should. He raced through it and did it sloppily.

- Sue knew her sister needed her help, but she just kept watching TV.

- Dan is very respectful towards his teachers.

- Peter likes to make fun of his classmates.

- Ann always has good things to say about others.

- Mary pays close attention in class and always does her chores at home.

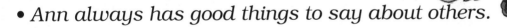

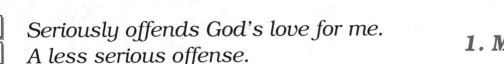

Write the correct number in the boxes on the left.

☐ Seriously offends God's love for me.
☐ A less serious offense.
☐ Separates a person from God.
☐ Seriously breaks God's Law.
☐ Can lead me to commit a mortal sin.
☐ Kills the Life of Grace within me.

1. Mortal sin

2. Venial sin

What I have learned

- Sin is the only thing that can take us away from God.
- Sin makes us lose our friendship with God.
- Sin kills within us the life of grace.
- Mortal sin is a serious offense towards God's love.
- Venial sin weakens my friendship with God.

What I will always remember

What is sin?
Sin is an offense against God's love, whom man disobeys when he does evil.

How many kinds of sin are there?
Two, mortal and venial.

What is mortal sin?
Mortal sin is a serious offense against God and kills the Life of Grace within us.

What is venial sin?
Venial sin is a less serious offense towards God that weakens our friendship with him.

What I am going to do

- I'm going to be extra careful not to hurt my friendship with Jesus by sinning
- I'm going to pray the Our Father every day asking God to help me resist temptations and always be close to him
- I'm also going to pray for my family and friends

God Is Always Ready to Forgive Us

Once we, the apostles, asked Jesus how often we had to forgive those who wronged us. He told us we had to forgive them always.

Do you always forgive those who wrong you?

Today we're going to learn there is one person who always forgives us.

A few parables Jesus told us

A father had two sons. One of them told him he wanted to leave home. The father became very sad because he loved the son very much. The son left and went far away.

Every day the father waited for his son to return, certain that he would come back someday. One day he finally saw him a long way off, coming down the road towards home. The father went off running to meet his son.

When he got to him he gave him a big hug, smiled, and laughed with joy, and welcomed his son back home, overjoyed to have him back.

There was a shepherd who had 100 sheep. He knew each one and loved them all.
One day one of his sheep got lost. So the shepherd put the other 99 and put them in their corral and went off in search of the one that got lost. It didn't matter that it was already late and getting cold. He kept looking until he found it. When he did, he petted it affectionately and brought it back to be with the rest of the flock. He was thrilled to have the sheep back again.

A woman once lost a coin in her house and became very troubled because she needed it. So she swept her entire house, moving all her furniture around to do it. At last she found the coin.

She became very happy and went to tell her friends that she had found the coin she'd lost.

Answer the questions.

1. How did the father feel when the son left home?

_____

2. What did the father do every day?

_____

3. What did he do when he saw his son coming home?

_____

4. How did he feel when he had his son back home?

_____

5. How did the woman feel when she lost her coin?

_____

6. What did she do when she found it?

_____

7. How may sheep did the shepherd have?

_____

8. How many sheep got lost?

_____

9. What did the shepherd do when one of his sheep got lost?

_____

10. What did he do when he found it?

_____

11. Why was he so happy to find his lost sheep?

_____

We are like the sheep, the coin, and the son.
When we sin, we drift away from God.
But he always comes looking for us, anxious to forgive us.

Color the paths connecting the boxes, and fill in the empty boxes with the pictures that should be there.

God is our Father. He loves us and always forgives us.
He is very happy when we return to him,
asking him to forgive us.

We mean a lot to God

Think of something that means a lot to you.
If you lose it, don't you go looking for it until you find it?

We all mean a great deal to God. He wants us all to be very happy and reach heaven. That's why he is always ready to forgive us.

Glue a photo of yourself here.

For God, this is a priceless treasure, and he doesn't want to lose it.

God's love for us is immense. He always offers us his forgiveness whenever we drift away from him through sin.

Following the color scheme given, color in the graph showing how much God loves us.

totally_____

a lot _____

somewhat _____

a little_____

Do the same thing here, showing how often God is willing to forgive us when we sin.

always_____

almost always_____

sometimes _____

never _____

Fill in the blanks.

sinning - Father - God - life - forgive - heaven

God is my _____. He gave me _____ and loves me very much.
I mean a great deal to _____. He wants me to be happy and wants me to get to _____.
When I turn away from God by _____, he is always ready to _____ me because he is my Father who loves me very much.

113

one hundred thirteen

What I have learned

- God is my Father and he loves me.
- I mean a great deal to God.
- When we sin we turn away from God, our Father.
- God is always ready to forgive us because he wants us to be happy and wants us to reach heaven.

What I will always remember

Why does Jesus say that God is like a loving father?

Because God loves us and is always ready to forgive us our failings.

What I am going to do

- I'm going to go to the chapel to thank God for how much he loves me, and to ask him to help me never to turn away from him.
- I'm going to be happy from now on because now I know that I am one of God's priceless treasures.

The Sacrament of Forgiveness

Jesus knows us very well and knows that there would be times when we will drift away from him through sin.
So he instituted a very special sacrament.

Our friend Jesus left us a very great gift that enables us always to be very close to God.

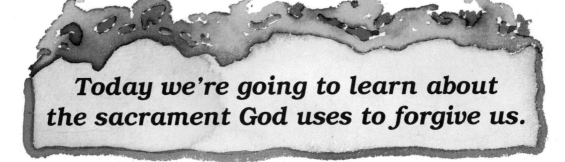

Today we're going to learn about the sacrament God uses to forgive us.

Easter Sunday

One afternoon during the first Easter season, all the apostles were in one place. Suddenly Jesus appeared and stood before them.

Jesus breathed on the apostles and said,

"Receive the Holy Spirit. Whose ever sins you forgive, they are forgiven them. Whose ever sins you do not forgive, they are not forgiven them."

Color the drawing and write what Jesus said to his apostles.

This was how Jesus instituted the Sacrament of Penance and Reconciliation, by which God forgives us the sins we commit after Baptism.

What is the Sacrament of Penance and Reconciliation?

Through the Sacrament of Penance and Reconciliation (or Confession), we regain the life of grace in our souls and become God's friends again.

The sacrament of Penance and Reconciliation...

• *brings us forgiveness for sins committed after Baptism.*

• *gives us strength to resist temptation.*

• *brings us back into friendship with God.*

• *must be received when we have committed a mortal sin.*

• *is the way God forgives us our sins, through a priest.*

How does the sacrament of Penance and Reconciliation work?

- When you commit a sin, but you are sorry and want to ask God to forgive you, you go to a priest.
- The priest welcomes you and asks you to tell him your sins.
- That's when you tell him what you have done to offend God.
- The priest will then give you some advice to help you be a better friend of Jesus.
- At the end, the priest will give you a penance to perform and will give you what is called "absolution," that is, forgiveness. He says:

"I absolve you from your sins in the name of the Father, and of the Son, and of the Holy Spirit."

At that moment God forgives you your sins.

God welcomes you back as his friend, grace reenters your soul, and you receive new strength for resisting temptation and being a better friend of God.

Put numbers in the circles to show the steps of Penance and Reconciliation.

Answer the questions.

Who instituted the sacrament of Penance and Reconciliation?

_____

When should we receive the sacrament of Penance and Reconciliation?

_____

Who forgives us our sins in God's name?

_____

What does the sacrament of Penance and Reconciliation give back to us?

_____

What I will always remember

- Jesus instituted the sacrament of Penance and Reconciliation (or Confession), by which God forgives us the sins we've committed after Baptism.
- Through the sacrament of Penance and Reconciliation we regain the Life of Grace and friendship with God.
- We should approach the sacrament of Penance and Reconciliation with great love and confidence.

What I will learn

What is the sacrament of Penance and Reconciliation?
It is the sacrament by which the sins we have committed after Baptism are forgiven.

Who instituted the sacrament of Penance and Reconciliation?
Jesus Christ instituted this sacrament.

What are the effects of the sacrament of Penance and Reconciliation?
Our sins are forgiven, we receive strength to resist temptation, we become God's friends again, and we regain the Life of Grace.

Who gives us the sacrament of Penance and Reconciliation?
A Catholic priest, who takes the place of Jesus Christ.

What I am going to do

- I'm going to say a special prayer to thank God for the great gift of the sacrament of Penance and Reconciliation, which enables me to be his friend again if I happen to sin.
- If I have already made my First Communion, I'm going to go to Confession again full of confidence and love.

Making a Good Confession

Jesus left us apostles with the mission of forgiving sins through the sacrament of Penance and Reconciliation. This sacrament is a great gift from God, one that we should all make the most of in order to be close to God and reach heaven.

When you're getting ready to go to a priest for Confession, do you know what you need to do to prepare yourself?

Today we're going to learn how to prepare ourselves to receive the sacrament of Penance and Reconciliation.

The Prodigal Son

Do you remember the parable of the prodigal son?

The prodigal son left home and his father because he wanted to go far away.

Then, far from home, he spent all his money, and didn't have enough to eat.

So he got a job feeding and taking care of pigs.

Draw the prodigal son taking care of the pigs.

After a while the prodigal son realized he'd made a big mistake and regretted leaving home. He decided to go back to his father and ask for forgiveness.
The father forgave his son and was very happy to have him home again.

Draw the prodigal son going home, and his father waiting for him.

Reflect and respond:

Why did the prodigal son go back to his father? _____

_____

How did the father feel when the son came back home? _____

_____

Why was the father so happy? _____

_____

Who is the father in this parable? _____

_____

Who is the son? _____

_____

How does God treat us when we go back to him? _____

_____

**Jesus left us a precious gift,
the sacrament of Penance and Reconciliation.**

Thanks to this sacrament, we can become God's friends again whenever we turn away from him by sinning.
Confession requires three steps.

Follow the trail between the boxes and you'll discover the meaning of each step.

1. Contrition or sorrow for my sins and decision not to sin again.	Jesus left priests in charge of forgiving sins in his name, personally representing him.
2. Confession or telling my sins to a priest.	Sin is an offense against God's love for me and so I should feel very sorry for every sin I have committed.
3. Satisfaction or penance.	Listening to the advice the priest gives me and enthusiastically carrying out the penance he gives me as a way to make up for the sins I have committed.

Satisfaction or penance means fulfilling what the priest asks me to do to make up for my sins.

The prodigal son followed these three steps, too.

Draw a line between each step of confession on the right with how the prodigal Son carried it out.

- The prodigal son examined his conscience and wasn't afraid to admit that he had done wrong. Remembering how he had acted, he realized he had sinned and offended his father.

- The son felt sorry for having offended his father who had always cared for him and treated him with love.

- The son decided to return home and do whatever he had to do to be a good son.

- The son asked his father to forgive him, telling him how he had offended him.

- The father forgave his son, and the son accepted following the rules of his house. The son asked his father to treat him as one of his servants in order to make up for the evil he had done.

A promise to make amends.

Telling one's sins to a priest.

Examination of conscience.

Reparation and fulfilling the penance given.

Sorrow for one's sins.

It is necessary to make a good examination of conscience before going to Confession.
How do I examine my conscience?

Examining your conscience is very important so that you'll know what you're going to say to the priest when you go to confession. But even before that, you need to feel very sorry for having offended God. You need to tell him how much you love him and that you never want to offend him again because he is your Father and loves you very much.

I need to examine my conscience in a quiet place where I can concentrate and not distracted by other things or other people. I need to think about God, asking him to help me because he is the one I have offended and the one who is going to forgive me. I need to thinkabout the ways I have acted in the different areas of my life: as a Catholic Christian, as a son or daughter, as a brother or sister, as a student, as a friend.

Here are some questions you can ask yourself to help make a good examination of conscience.

As a Catholic Christian
- *Have I thought about God, or only about myself?*
- *Have I tried to behave as God requests?*
- *Have I gone to Mass? How have I behaved during Mass?*
- *Have I prayed every day, as God requests?*
- *Have I ever acted out of envy or hatred, or have I always acted out of love?*

As a child
- *Have I been obedient to and respectful of my parents, just as Jesus teaches?*
- *Do I help my parents whenever they ask me to help?*
- *Have I shown my parents how much I love them?*
- *Do I listen carefully to what they tell me?*

As a brother or sister

- Am I happy and affectionate with my brothers and sisters, just as Jesus has taught me?
- Do I lend them my things and help them when I can?
- Do I like to get along with them, or do I look for every chance to fight with them?

As a student

- Am I respectful of and obedient to my teachers, just as Jesus requests?
- Have I always done all my homework?
- Do I use my time well, putting my best effort into my school projects?

As a friend

- Am I a good friend to others, just as Jesus wants requests?
- Do I happily share my things with my friends?
- Am I easy to get along with, or do I always insist on getting my own way?
- Do I ever make fun of my friends?

During Confession, before receiving absolution, you need to pray this prayer:

Act of Contrition

My God,
I am sorry for my sins with all my heart.
In choosing to do wrong and failing to do good,
I have sinned against you
whom I should love above all things.
I firmly intend, with your help,
to do penance, to sin no more,
and to avoid whatever leads me to sin.

Our Savior Jesus Christ
suffered and died for us.
In his name, my God, have mercy.

What I have learned

- The sacrament of Penance and Reconciliation is a great gift Jesus gave us. Through it our sins are forgiven and we are brought back into friendship with God.
- We need to prepare ourselves very well for each and every confession.
- Every time we go to confession we regain our friendship with God, if we have had the misfortune of losing it.

What I will always remember

What are the steps to making a good confession?
There are three steps to making a good confession:
1. Contrition or sorrow for my sins and the decision not to sin again.
2. Confession or telling my sins to a priest.
3. Satisfaction or penance, which means willfully fulfilling what the priest asks me to do to make up for my sins.

What is an examination of conscience?
The examination of conscience is recalling the sins I have committed since my last confession.

What is "sorrow for one's sins"?
It's admitting that I have offended God and being sorry for it.

What is "firm purpose of amendment"?
It's having the firm intention of not sinning again and taking the necessary steps to avoid sinning.

What is "telling my sins to a priest"?
This means sincerely and humbly telling the priest the sins I've committed since my last confession.

What is "satisfaction or penance"?
It is recovering my spiritual health by doing something more to make up for my sins by willfully fulfilling what the priest asks me to do. It means carrying out the penance the priest assigns me in Confession in order to make up for my sins.

What I am going to do

- Every time I go to Confession I'm going to make a special effort to prepare myself for it by following all the steps for making a good confession.

Jesus Comes to Save Us from Our Sins

Jesus came to earth with a very special mission, and he was always very careful to do everything necessary to fulfill it.
His great mission was to save us from sin and to bring us back into friendship with God.

You, too, have a mission.
Do you know what it is?

Today we're going to learn that Jesus always did his Father's will.

What Jesus did to fulfill his mission

Jesus is born
Jesus began his mission by being born in a simple stable in the town of Bethlehem.

Hidden life in Nazareth
Jesus grew up in Nazareth where he was always obedient to Joseph and Mary, learning all that they had to teach him.

Public life
Jesus began his public life by calling the disciples and then going about teaching everyone the way to be happy and reach heaven.

Passion and death

Jesus died on the cross out of love for us, to save us from sin, and bring us back into friendship with God.

Resurrection and Ascension

Jesus overcame death and sin. He came back to life and ascended to heaven to be with his Father. From there, he helps us on our way to heaven.

In all things, at every moment of his life, Jesus always did the will of his Father. He always and everywhere lovingly obedyed God, his Father.

Jesus' mission

Jesus came to earth to carry out a great mission.

Through his life, death, and resurrection Jesus saved us from sin, brought us back into friendship with God, and reopened the gates of heaven for us.

He did all of this to fulfill his Father's will, obeying with great love all that his Father asked of him.

Our mission

We, too, have a very great mission to carry out.

Using the colors of the titles on the left, color in the circle to show which person has the job, or mission, referred to on the right.

○ Takes care of us and loves us.

○ Helps us reach heaven.

Doctor

○ Tells us which medicine to take.

○ Teaches us new things.

Teacher

○ Gives us the sacraments.

Mother

○ Makes sure we have everything we need at home.

○ Treats us when we are sick.

Priest

○ Helps us to study better.

What is your mission?

In the space provided write what you think you have to do to fulfill your misison...

As a son or daughter:_____
_____

As a student:_____
_____

As a brother or sister: _____
_____

As a friend:_____
_____

As a child of God: _____
_____

How are you going to go about fulfilling your mission?

**The key to fulfilling your mission is
to always do what God asks of us,
fulfilling his will at all times
with great love and joy,
just as Jesus did.**

Fill in the blanks.

obey - friendship - will - mission - love

Jesus came to earth to carry out a _____: to save us from
sin and bring us back into _____ with God.
Jesus always did God's _____ full of _____.
We, too must always _____ the will of God.

What I have learned

- Jesus came to earth to carry out a mission: to save us from sin and bring us back into friendship with God.
- Jesus always did the will of his Father out of great love for him.
- We, too, have a mission to fulfill.
- We should fulfill our mission with great love and a deep desire to obey God in all things.

What I will always remember

Why did Jesus come to earth?
To save us from sin and bring us back into friendship with God.

In what way did Jesus carry out his mission?
With great love, always doing the will of his Father.

What I am going to do

- Out of obedience and love, I'm going to do whatever God asks of me, especially the things I find hardest.

The Last Supper

Have you ever been to a dinner where something very special was being celebrated?

We apostles ate with Jesus often, but there was one meal we shared with him that was very special.

Today we're going to recall Jesus' Last Supper with his disciples.

A Special Meal

On Holy Thursday night Jesus met with his disciples to celebrate the Passover meal. After the meal Jesus did something new and very special.

Taking some bread he said, "Take this all of you and eat it. This is my body, which will be given up for you."

Then taking a cup of wine he said, "Take this all of you and drink from it. This is the cup of my blood, the blood of the new and everlasting covenant. It will be shed for you and for all so that sins may be forgiven."

Then he said to his disciples, "Do this in memory of me." It was at that moment that Jesus instituted the sacrament of the Eucharist.

Carefully answer the questions.

With whom was Jesus eating?_____
_____

What were they celebrating?_____
_____

What did Jesus do after the meal?_____
_____

What did he turn the bread into?_____
_____

What did he turn the wine into?_____
_____

What did he say to his disciples afterwards?_____
_____

What sacrament did Jesus institute at the Last Supper? _____
_____

Why was the Last Supper so special?_____
_____

At the Last Supper Jesus left us a very great gift,
the sacrament of the Eucharist

> **The Sacrament of the Eucharist is the Body and Blood of Christ under the appearances of bread and wine. It was instituted at the Last Supper.**

The Eucharist is the sacrament of Christ's love.
He loves us so much that he came up with a way to stay with us forever.

He instituted the sacrament of the Eucharist and is always with us in the Tabernacle.

Color the tabernacle. Don't forget to color the candle red, showing that Jesus is present in the tabernacle in the sacrament of the Eucharist. Fill in the picture by drawing children visiting Jesus in the Tabernacle.

Jesus, your very best friend, is waiting for you in the tabernacle.

In the space provided write how you think you should behave when you are in front of or near the tabernacle.

_____

_____

_____

_____

Visiting Jesus in the Eucharist

Jesus stayed with us in the Eucharist and he wants us to visit him there as often as we can.

When you visit Jesus in the Eucharist:

Tell him how much you love him.

Write a short prayer telling Jesus you love him.

_____

_____

_____

_____

_____

Thank him.

What do you have to thank Jesus for?

_____

_____

_____

Adore him.
since he's your God and Savior.

Ask him for the things you need.
Think for a moment about what things you need for which you can ask Jesus.

Pray for others

In the space below write the names of those for whom you can pray to Jesus:

_____

_____

A New Commandment

At the Last Supper Jesus gave us a new commandment. He wants all of us who are his friends to live according to this new commandment.

In the square, glue lots of pictures of people from all over the world. Then color in Jesus' new commandment.

If we are Jesus' friends, we ought to keep his new commandment by truly loving one another.

"Love one another as I have loved you."

What do we need to do to live according to Jesus' new commandment?

Find the words below in this alphabet soup. They are ways you can keep Jesus' commandment and be his friend.

H	E	L	P	A	G	H	Q	W	O	R
A	S	D	R	M	N	D	U	I	B	X
G	K	E	A	C	Z	J	K	L	E	A
V	Q	W	Y	T	U	P	L	X	Y	S
D	V	Y	F	O	R	G	I	V	E	H
B	Q	C	O	N	S	O	L	E	S	A
K	L	M	R	V	B	C	X	A	S	R
R	E	S	P	E	C	T	F	K	L	E

help • respect • obey • share • forgive • pray for • console

Fill in the blanks using the drawings as clues.

Jesus stays with us under the appearances of _____ and

_____ in the sacrament of the Eucharist. He shows

us his great _____ for us.

We can visit him in the _____ every day.

In the space provided, write Jesus' new commandment:

_____

_____

What I have learned

- Jesus instituted the sacrament of the Eucharist at the Last Supper, when he turned bread and wine into his own Body and Blood.
- Jesus has stayed with us in the tabernacle, where we can visit him to tell him how much we love him, thank him, and adore him.
- At the Last Supper Jesus gave us his new commandment, to love one another as he has loved us.

What I will always remember

What is the sacrament of the Eucharist?
It is the sacrament of the Body and Blood of Christ under the appearances of bread and wine.

When did Jesus institute the sacrament of the Eucharist?
At the Last Supper.

Why should we visit Jesus in the Eucharist?
To tell him that we love him, adore him, and thank him.

What is Jesus' new commandment?
"Love one another as I have loved you."

What I am going to do

- I'm going to go to the chapel to visit Jesus in the tabernacle to thank him for the great gift of the Eucharist.
- I'm going to invite a friend to do the same.
- At night I'm going to ask myself honestly if I have lived my day following Jesus' new commandment, loving others as Jesus loves me.

Jesus' Sacrifice

Jesus showed us how much he loves us by taking upon himself an immense sacrifice. He did it to save us from sin and bring us back into friendship with God.
Thanks to that sacrifice we are now able to reach heaven.

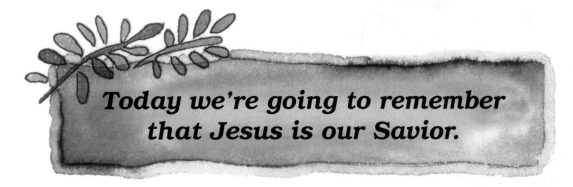

Today we're going to remember that Jesus is our Savior.

Holy Week

Do you remember what happened during Holy Week?

Put the events in order by writing the correct number in each circle.

Jesus accepted his passion and death out of love for his Father and out of love for us, to save us from sin and give us eternal life.

Following the "Way of the Cross"

The "Via Crucis," or "Way of the Cross," helps us to remember the different moments Jesus had to live through in his passion, from being condemned to death to being laid in the tomb. The different moments are called "stations," which is why the Via Crucis is also called the "Stations of the Cross."

Study each station below. You can use this guide to help you pray the stations with your family on Good Friday. In the blue boxes write down what you're going to do to be very close to Jesus during Holy Week.

1. Jesus is condemned to death.

2. Jesus carries his cross.

3. Jesus falls the first time.

4. Jesus meets his mother.

5. Simon of Cyrene helps Jesus.

6. Veronica wipes the face of Jesus.

7. Jesus falls the second time.

13 Jesus is taken down from the cross.

14 Jesus is laid in the tomb.

2 Jesus dies on the cross.

10 Jesus is stripped of his garments.

11 Jesus is nailed to the cross.

8 Jesus consoles the holy women.

9 Jesus falls the third time.

What I have learned

- Jesus came to earth to save us. He is our Savior.
- Through his sacrifice on the cross, Jesus saved us from sin and brought us back into friendship with God.
- Jesus accepted the sacrifice of the cross out of love for us and to fulfill his Father's will.
- We can help Jesus bring more people to heaven by performing good works out of love for God.

What I will always remember

Why did Jesus die on the cross?
To save us from sin, to open for us the way to eternal life, and to show us how we are to obey God's will.

What did Jesus achieve by dying on the cross?
By dying for us, Jesus won our salvation.

What I am going to do

- To help Jesus in his mission as Savior, I'm going to do my homework and carry out my school responsibilities the best I can, out of love for God.
- I'm going to visit Jesus in the tabernacle to thank him for loving me so much.

The Sacrifice of The Mass

We apostles were able to be with Jesus as he sacrificed himself to save us from sin. Jesus also decided to leave us a way to relive his sacrifice so that all of you could participate in it, too. Do you know what we call this celebration?

Today we're going to find out about Jesus' very own celebration.

"Do this in memory of me."

_____
_____
_____
_____

_____
_____
_____
_____

_____
_____
_____
_____

_____
_____
_____
_____

Answer the questions.

How is Jesus present? _____

_____

What is the priest doing?_____

_____

_____

At the Holy Mass both the Last Supper and Jesus' sacrifice on the cross are relived.

The Holy Mass

At the Holy Mass we gather to celebrate the reliving of the Last Supper and Jesus' sacrifice on the cross.

Holy Mass can be divided into two main parts:

- **Liturgy of the Word**
- **Liturgy of the Eucharist**

Liturgy of the Word

- *We listen to God's Word, written down in the **Bible**.*

- *We learn about Jesus' life and teachings in the **Gospels**.*

- *The readings and Gospel are explained to us by the priest during the **Homily**.*

- *We pray together for the needs of the Church during the **Prayers of the faithful**.*

Liturgy of the Eucharist

The Liturgy of the Eucharist
is the reliving of Jesus'
sacrifice on the cross.

• We offer God gifts of bread and
wine during the **Offertory.**

• The bread and wine become
the Body and Blood of Christ
when the priest says the words
of **Consecration.**

• We receive Jesus himself,
under the appearances of bread
and wine, in **Holy Communion.**

Living the Holy Mass

To live the Holy Mass and join Jesus in this his celebration, we should

Listen carefully to what Jesus wants to say to us
during the readings and homily.
Offer our lives to God as Jesus offers himself to his Father.
Unite ourselves to Jesus during Holy Communion.

**Which part of the Mass does each photograph show?
Write your answer under the photograph.**

20

We should be very respectful throughout Mass, sit, stand, or kneel depending on the part of Mass being celebrated.

These three postures stand for different ways of participating at Mass: Follow the dotted lines to find out what each posture stands for.

Participate by adoring our God and Savior.

Seated.

Participate by carefully listening, just as Jesus' disciples listened to him.

Standing.

Kneeling.

Participate by being ready to hear and respond to God's call.

Match the two columns by writing the correct number from the left in its corresponding circle on the right.

1. Holy Mass
2. Liturgy of the Word and Liturgy of the Eucharist
3. Listening, offering ourselves, receiving Communion
4. The Bible
5. The Gospel
6. The homily
7. Prayer of the Faithful
8. Offertory
9. Consecration
10. Holy Communion
11. Standing
12. Kneeling
13. Seated

○ Participating by listening carefully.
○ Praying together for the needs of the Church.
○ Receiving Jesus under the appearances of bread and wine.
○ Two parts of the Mass.
○ Participating by being ready to listen and respond.
○ Reliving the Last Supper and Jesus' sacrifice on the cross.
○ The priest explains the readings.
○ Participating by adoring.
○ God's written word.
○ Spoken by the priest to turn the bread and wine into the Body and Blood of Christ.
○ Ways of living the Mass.
○ The life and teachings of Jesus.
○ We offer to God the bread and wine.

What I have learned

- We Catholic Christians gather together to celebrate the Holy Mass.
- The Holy Mass is the reliving of the Last Supper and Jesus' sacrifice on the cross.
- We should participate in Mass with great attention and love since it is the celebration of Jesus, our friend, and Savior.

What I will always remember

What is the Holy Mass?
The Holy Mass is the gathering of Catholic Christians to celebrate the reliving of the Last Supper and Christ's sacrifice on the cross.

What are the two main parts of the Mass?
The Liturgy of the Word and the Liturgy of the Eucharist.

How can we "live" the Holy Mass?
We can live the Mass by:
- Carefully listening to Jesus' message throughout each part of the Mass.
- Offering our lives to God as Jesus offers himself to the Father
- Uniting ourselves to Jesus in Holy Communion

What are the postures we should assume during Mass?
- Standing, ready to respond to God's call
- Kneeling, in adoration
- Seated, carefully listening

What I am going to do

- I'm going to make a very special effort to live the Holy Mass very close to Jesus, by paying attention.
- I'm going to help my brothers, sisters, and friends live the Mass close to Jesus, too, by setting a good example for them.

Jesus Speaks to Us at Mass

Jesus talked with us apostles often.
He taught us the way to heaven.
He spent time talking to a lot of other
people, too, always teaching them about
God and heaven. We all listened to him very carefully.

When someone who loves you a lot talks to you, what do you do?

Today we're going to be reminded that we should listen very carefully when Jesus speaks to us.

Jesus once said

"My words are words of eternal life!"

This means that if we listen to what Jesus says to us and follow his teachings, we'll reach heaven.

Great crowds of people followed Jesus to hear him speak. They must have listened very carefully, paying close attention so as not to miss a single word. That made it possible for them to put into practice everything Jesus said.

All these people are listening to Jesus' words.
Find in the picture:

- A boy dressed in blue paying very close attention.
- A girl with a flower in her hand.
- A man standing up, listening very carefully.
- A woman holding a child in her arms.
- St. John the Evangelist with a pen in his hand.
- Three birds.
- Two sheep.

Everybody listened carefully to Jesus because they knew his words would teach them the way to heaven.

What about you? How carefully do you listen to God's word?

The Liturgy of the Word

During the Holy Mass we hear the word of God written in the **Bible**.

**The Bible is God's written word.
It's divided into two parts,
the Old Testament and the New Testament.**

**The Liturgy of the Word has
the following parts:**
- **The first reading**
- **The Responsorial psalm**
- **The second reading**
- **The Gospel**
- **The homily**
- **The Prayer of the faithful**

First Reading

*This reading is from the first part
of the Bible, the* **Old Testament**.

Responsorial Psalm

*The Psalms are songs written in
praise of God. They are found in
the* **Old Testament**.

Second Reading

*This reading is from the letters
written by Jesus' apostles. These
letters are found in the* **New
Testament**.

The Gospel

This is the most important part of the Liturgy of the Word. The Gospels record the life and teachings of Jesus. We stand up to listen to the Gospel.

The Homily

The priest explains the readings and the Gospel so that we can follow Jesus' teachings more closely.

Prayer of the Faithful

In the prayer of the faithful we join together to pray for our needs and the needs of the Church and the world.

Pay close attention during the Liturgy of the Word next Sunday, and then answer the following questions.

From which book of the Bible was the first reading?_____

_____

What response was used during the responsorial psalm?_____

_____

From which book of the Bible was the second reading?_____

_____

What was your favorite part of the Gospel?_____

_____

What did the priest say in his homily?_____

_____

For whom did you pray for during the Prayer of the faithful?_____

_____

Getting to know the word of God

God speaks to you through his word during the Mass, but you can read the Bible at home, too.

In the Bible God tells you how much he loves you and how you need to act to reach heaven.

Let's learn to read the Bible!

Here is a page from the Bible. Pay close attention to the different parts.

This tells you which book of the Bible you're reading.

These numbers tell you chapters you will find on this page. They also help you find the beginning of each chapter.

Mark 10-11

13 And people were bringing children to him that he might touch them, but the disciples rebuked them.
14 When Jesus saw this he became indignant and said to them, "Let the children come to me; do not prevent them, for the kingdom of God belongs to such as these. 15 "Amen, I say to you, whoever does not accept the kingdom of God like a child will not enter it."
16 Then he embraced them and blessed them, placing his hands on them.

These little numbers mark what are called verses. They help you find specific passages.

Draw a blue circle around the name of the book. Draw a green circle around the chapter numbers on this page. Draw red circles around all the verse numbers you find.

Here is a short reading from St. Luke's Gospel.

Underline with a red pen verses 6 and 7 from chapter 15.

Luke 15

3 So to them he addressed this parable.

4 What man among you having a hundred sheep and losing one of them would not leave the ninety-nine in the desert and go after the lost one until he finds it?

5 And when he does find it, he sets it on his shoulders with great joy

6 and, upon his arrival home, he calls together his friends and neighbors and says to them, 'Rejoice with me because I have found my lost sheep.'

7 "I tell you, in just the same way there will be more joy in heaven over one sinner who repents than over ninety-nine righteous people who have no need of repentance."

If the statement is true, color the Bible green. If it's false, color it red.

- The Liturgy of the Word is part of Holy Mass.
- The Bible is God's written Word.
- The consecration is part of the Liturgy of the word.
- The Bible is divided into the Old and New Testaments.
- The psalms are songs in praise of God.
- The Gospel tells us about the life of St. Paul.
- The Gospel is explained during the homily.
- The letters of the apostles are read during the prayer of the faithful.

What I have learned

- We should listen carefully to what Jesus says to us.
- God talks to us at Mass during the Liturgy of the Word.
- At Mass we listen to the Word of God written in the Bible.
- We should pay close attention to what God wants to say to us at each Mass.
- The Liturgy of the Word is made up of the first reading, the responsorial psalm, the Gospel, the homily, and the prayer of the faithful.

What I will always remember

What are the main parts of the Liturgy of the Word?
The readings, the responsorial psalm, the Gospel, the homily, and the Prayer of the Faithful.

What is the most important part of the Liturgy of the Word?
The Gospel because it contains the life and teachings of Jesus.

What I am going to do

- I'm going to be very attentive at Sunday Mass so as not to miss what God wants to tell me in the Liturgy of the Word.
- At home, I'm going to take a few minutes every day to read about Jesus in the Gospels.

Offering Our Lives to God

Jesus offered himself to his Father out of love for us. Through his life, Jesus showed us how we should be ready to offer all that we have to God, out of love for others.

What do you have to offer to someone who loves you very much?

Today we're going to learn that we have a lot we can offer to God.

Jesus offered his very life to God his Father

Jesus offered himself up to his Father as a sacrifice of love. He wanted to save us from sin and bring us back into friendship with God.

Color this drawing and underneath it write what you can remember about Jesus' sacrifice.

_____

_____

_____

The Offertory

During Mass the priest offers bread and wine to God so that they may become the Body and Blood of Jesus.

God gives us the wheat and the grapes. Men make it into bread and wine. During Mass the priest offers them up to God.

We can offer ourselves, too

Jesus offered his entire life to God.
We can do the same thing, offering to God everything we do out of love for him and to help Jesus bring more and more people to heaven.

In the space provided write three things you do at home:

_____

_____

Three things you do at school:

_____

_____

Three things you do with your friends:

_____

_____

You can do all these things with great love and offer them to God

Write on the paten below what you are going to offer to God during the offertory of the Mass this coming Sunday.

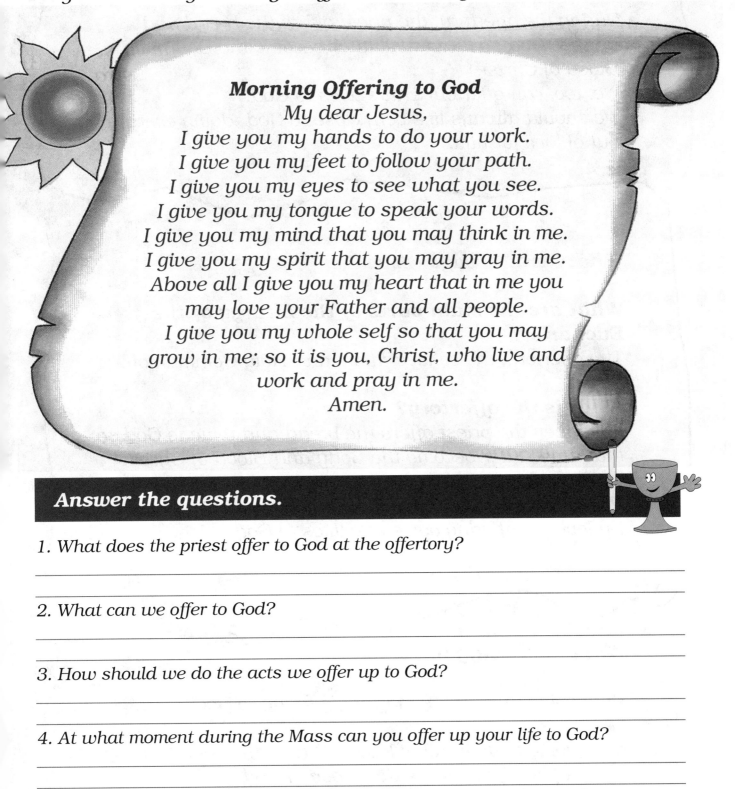

You can offer your entire life to God
Pray to God every morning to offer him the day ahead.

Morning Offering to God
My dear Jesus,
I give you my hands to do your work.
I give you my feet to follow your path.
I give you my eyes to see what you see.
I give you my tongue to speak your words.
I give you my mind that you may think in me.
I give you my spirit that you may pray in me.
Above all I give you my heart that in me you
may love your Father and all people.
I give you my whole self so that you may
grow in me; so it is you, Christ, who live and
work and pray in me.
Amen.

Answer the questions.

1. What does the priest offer to God at the offertory?

_____

_____

2. What can we offer to God?

_____

_____

3. How should we do the acts we offer up to God?

_____

_____

4. At what moment during the Mass can you offer up your life to God?

_____

_____

What I have learned

- During the offertory, the priest offers the bread and wine to God so that it will later become the Body and Blood of Christ.
- We, too, can offer our entire lives to God.
- We should always live very close to God, doing everything out of love for him.

What I will always remember

What are the main parts of the Liturgy of the Eucharist?
The offertory, the consecration, and Holy Communion.

What is the offertory?
It is when the priest offers the bread and wine to God so that it will later become the Body and Blood of Christ.

How can we participate in the offertory?
By lovingly offering our entire lives to God.

What I am going to do

- I'm going to pray the morning offering to God every day.
- I'm going to do it full of love and with the goal of living my entire day close to God.

The Words of Consecration

When we apostles were with Jesus at the Last Supper and he turned bread and wine into his own Body and Blood, he told us that from then on we should do the same in memory of him.
So now, every time Mass is celebrated anywhere in the world, the priest repeats exactly what Christ did at the Last Supper.
Do you know at what point of the Mass the priest does this?

Today we're going to learn about the most important part of the Mass.

"Do this in memory of me"

These were Christ's words at the Last Supper after he had turned the bread and wine into his Body and Blood.

It was then that Christ celebrated the first Mass, and he instructed his apostles and their successors, Catholic priests, to do the same.

Finish the drawing.
Draw yourself at the Last Supper with Jesus.
Draw your friends, too, or the people you love most.

Now finish this drawing. Draw yourself, friends, and family attending Holy Mass.

The events that occurred at the Last Supper occur again at every Mass.

When the priest repeats Jesus' words from the Last Supper, the bread and wine become the Body and Blood of Christ. This happens during the Consecration.

Underneath the drawings write how they are alike.

"Take this all of you and eat it. This is my Body which will be given up for you."

"Take this all of you and drink from it. This is the cup of my Blood, the Blood of the new and everlasting covenant. It will be shed for you and for all so that sins may be forgiven. Do this in memory of me."

_____

_____

_____

_____

Do this in memory of me.

The consecration is the central moment of the Mass

We should pay very close attention during the **consecration**. Aware that Christ is coming to be with us in the sacrament of the Eucharist, we should humbly adore him on our knees.

Study the photograph and answer the questions.

Describe the photograph above.

_____

Who is consecrating the bread and wine?

_____

What are they being turned into?

_____

Are those attending this Mass sitting, standing, or kneeling at this point?

_____

What I have learned

- The consecration is the central moment of the Mass.
- During the consecration the priest repeats Christ's words from the Last Supper, and the bread and wine become the Body and Blood of Christ.
- During the consecration we should show great love and respect for Jesus in the sacrament of the Eucharist.

What I will always remember

What is the consecration?

It is the moment during the Mass when, through the priest's words, the bread and wine become the Body and Blood of Christ.

What are the words the priest says during the consecration?

The same words Christ spoke at the Last Supper when he turned the bread and wine into his Body and Blood.

What should we be doing during the consecration?

Paying close attention, kneeling to adore Christ who comes to be with us in the sacrament of the Eucharist.

What I am going to do

- I'm always going to be very attentive during the consecration whenever I go to Mass, showing Christ great love and respect.
- I will be careful not to get distracted with other thoughts or things, and am going to help my friends and all those around me to do the same.

Holy Communion

Jesus was always ready to help anyone in need. Once he even fed a large number of people who were following him. They had been with him all day and he knew they were hungry.

Jesus said he would give us food, too, food for our souls to help us reach heaven.

Today we're going to learn about the Bread of Life that Jesus gives us.

The miracle of the loaves and fishes

One day many people had gone with Jesus to hear him speak.

Since they were with Jesus for a long time, the people began to get hungry and didn't have enough food. There were only five loaves of bread and two fish for the entire crowd.

Jesus told his disciples to hand out the loaves and fish to the people. As they handed them out, they realized that the loaves and fish didn't run out.

Somehow there was more than enough. Everyone ate and there were even 12 baskets of bread and fish left over.

Using colored paper, cut out loaves and fish to fill the baskets that were left over after the miracle of the loaves and fish.

Just as Jesus fed all these people, he gives us food for our souls.

I am the Bread of Life

Jesus once said:

*"I am the Bread of Life.
Whoever eats this bread shall
live forever."*

HEAVEN

6. temptation

5. venial

4. Grace

3. souls

2. Catholic Christians

1. Christ

What happens when we receive Holy Communion?

The food Christ was talking about is the sacrament of the Eucharist.
We receive this food in Holy Communion when we receive Jesus
under the appearances of bread and wine.

Fill in the blanks using the numbers on the steps leading to heaven. Then you'll find out what happens when we receive Communion and how it helps us reach heaven.

Holy Communion
Unites us to 1_____ and to the Church.
Forms a bond between all 2_____.
Nourishes our 3_____.
Increases within us the Life of 4_____ and
Strengthens our friendship with God.
Gains forgiveness of 5_____ sins.
Gives us strength to resist 6_____ and not to fall into
mortal sin.

Jesus is the Bread of Life.
We receive the Bread of Life in Holy Communion.

How often can we receive Holy Communion?

What effect does eating well have on boys and girls?
Write your answer below:

_____
_____
_____
_____

What effect does receiving Holy Communion every day have on boys and girls?

_____
_____
_____
_____

Just as our bodies need food every day, our souls need spiritual food, the Bread of Life. This is our nourishment for reaching heaven.

During Mass, we receive Chris in Holy Communion. You can receive him every day at church or at school.

In the space provided write some things you can offer up the next few times you receive Holy Communion.

_____
_____
_____
_____
_____
_____
_____

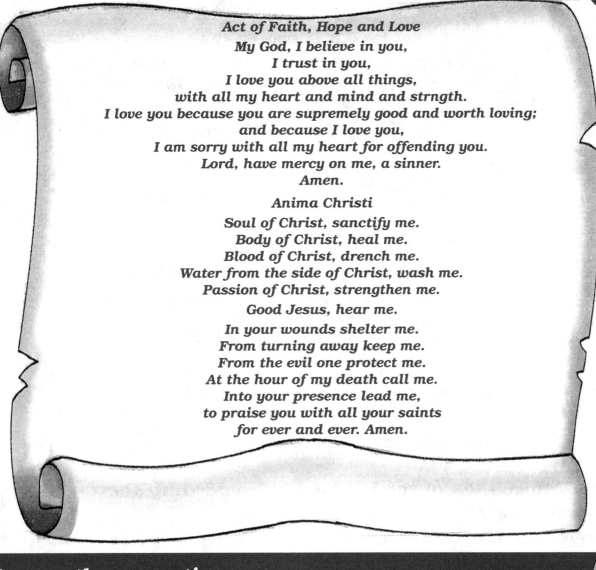

Act of Faith, Hope and Love

My God, I believe in you,
I trust in you,
I love you above all things,
with all my heart and mind and strngth.
I love you because you are supremely good and worth loving;
and because I love you,
I am sorry with all my heart for offending you.
Lord, have mercy on me, a sinner.
Amen.

Anima Christi

Soul of Christ, sanctify me.
Body of Christ, heal me.
Blood of Christ, drench me.
Water from the side of Christ, wash me.
Passion of Christ, strengthen me.

Good Jesus, hear me.

In your wounds shelter me.
From turning away keep me.
From the evil one protect me.
At the hour of my death call me.
Into your presence lead me,
to praise you with all your saints
for ever and ever. Amen.

Answer these questions.

1. What kind of food was Jesus talking about when he said, "I am the Bread of Life"?

_____

_____

2. To whom or what does Holy Communion unite us?

_____

_____

3. Why should we receive Holy Communion often?

_____

_____

What I have learned

- *Jesus gives us food for our souls.*
- *The food Jesus gives us is the sacrament of the Eucharist.*
- *We receive the Bread of Life during Mass, at the time of Holy Communion.*
- *We should receive Holy Communion often.*

What I will always remember

What is sacramental Communion?
Receiving Christ under the appearances of bread and wine.

What are the effects of Holy Communion?
- We are united to Christ and the Church
- Catholic Christians are united to one another
- Our souls are nourished
- Our souls grow in grace and friendship with God
- Venial sins are forgiven
- We receive strength against temptation and falling into mortal sin

What does the Church recommend regarding sacramental Communion?
It recommends that we receive Communion every time we go to Mass, unless we are in serious sin.

What I am going to do

- *I'm going to go to Communion every possible day this week, full of love and respect, thanking Christ for wanting to give me this food for my soul.*
- *After receiving Communion, I'm going to pray hard to Jesus, asking him to help all children know and love him.*
- *If I haven't made my first Communion yet, I'm going to go to the chapel <u>and</u> make a Spiritual Communion.*

Getting Ready to Receive Jesus

When it was about time for the Last Supper, Jesus told us apostles to get things ready. We made sure we had everything we needed for such a special occasion.

When something special is coming up, you, too, get everything ready the very best you can.

Today we're going to learn how we should get ready for participating in Jesus' own celebration.

The rude guest

One day Jesus told his friends a parable

Color the drawings.

There once was a very rich man who decided to hold a big feast. He invited people from all over because he had lots of friends.

When the day came, all those who were invited got ready, dressing up in their finest clothes.

But then at the feast, one fellow suddenly showed up all dirty, poorly dressed, and definitely in a bad mood.

So the man in charge of the feast told him he had to leave. No one as dirty or poorly dressed as he could attend the feast.

Answer the questions.

How did the people invited get ready for the feast?

_____

How did the rude guest show up?

_____

What did the host of the feast tell him?

_____

Why did he have to leave?

_____

Getting ready for a friend's birthday party

When a friend invites you to his or her birthday party, you should always look your best. Your mother will help you select your nicest clothes. Even though you'd like to wear your favorite pants and shirt, you should go to the party well groomed with appropriate clothing.

Draw a circle around the things you think are appropriate for a birthday party.

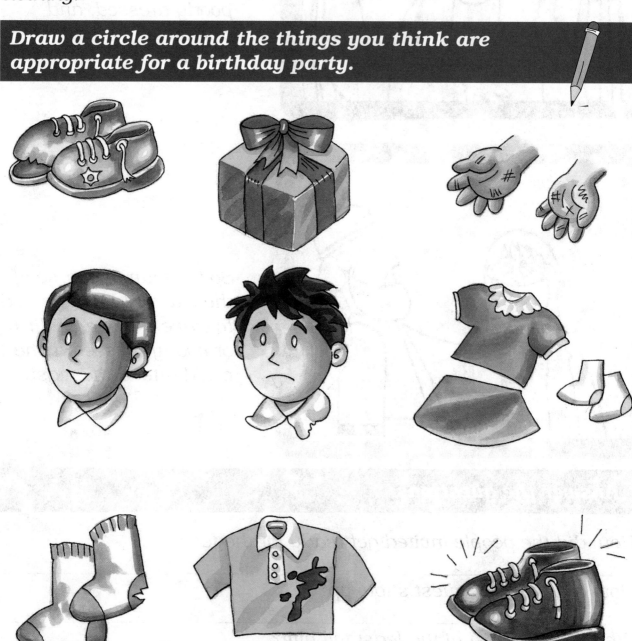

This is how you get ready for a birthday party. It's also how you should get ready for Jesus' celebration.

Jesus has invited you

He's invited you to his great celebration and to receive him in the sacrament of the Eucharist.

Answer the questions.

To what celebration has Jesus invited you?

_____

_____

What is the best way to get ready for Jesus' celebration?

_____

_____

What should your soul be like to participate in Jesus' celebration?

_____

_____

What is the only thing that can stain your soul?

_____

_____

Getting ready to receive Jesus for the first time

When you're going to receive Jesus for the first time, you get a lot of things ready

Your candle, which stands for the light that your faith in Jesus is going to give your whole life.

Rosary beads, so that you'll always remember Mary is your mother and will always help you on your way to heaven.

Jesus' Word, which will teach you how to be Jesus' true friend.

A crucifix, the sign of the Christian.

What other things help us get ready for First Communion?

Write them down here:

_____
_____
_____
_____
_____
_____ .

Above all, we need to prepare ourselves by studying our catechism, knowing Jesus and his life. We must do everything we can to stay far away from sin and very close to Jesus, to keep our souls clean.

Every time you receive Holy Communion at church or school you also have to get ready. Here are some things you need to do.

Match up the columns by coloring the chalice the correct color.

● State of Grace.

● Go to Confession.

● Fasting.

Not to eat any food or candy an hour before receiving Communion.

If I have committed a mortal sin.

Having my soul clean and being in friendship with God.

The most important thing is preparing your heart, and getting it ready to welcome Jesus, your Savior and very best friend.

Learn this prayer. Praying it will help you get ready to receive Jesus into your heart.

I confess to Almighty God, and to you my brothers and sisters, that I have sinned through my own fault, in my thoughts and in my words, in what I have done and what I have failed to do.
And I ask the Blessed Mary ever Virgin, all the angels and saints, and you, my brothers and sisters, to pray for me to the Lord, our God.

What I have learned

- Jesus invites me to his great celebration.
- I need to get ready for this celebration.
- To be ready to receive Jesus I need to be in the state of grace and fast for one hour beforehand.
- If I have committed a mortal sin I need to go to Confession before receiving Communion.

What I will always remember

What are the conditions for going to Communion?
Fasting and being in the state of grace.

What kind of fasting is required?
No food or drink for an hour before receiving Communion.

What I am going to do

- I'm always going to prepare myself very well for receiving Jesus in Holy Communion.
- On my way up to Communion, I'm going to concentrate on who I am about to receive, instead of playing around or thinking about other things.
- I'm going to help a friend to do this, too.
- After receiving Communion I'm going to be sure to thank God full of love and devotion.

Prayer

Jesus used to pray every day when we apostles were with him. He didn't let a single day go by without praying to his Father. By his example, he showed us that we, too, needed to pray every day.

He tells all of you that you also need to pray if you want to stay close to him and be his friend.

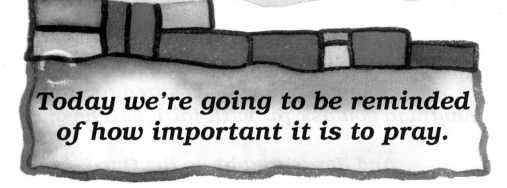

Today we're going to be reminded of how important it is to pray.

Jesus talked to us about prayer

Jesus knew how important it was for us to learn to pray.
We used to pray every day, just like he did.

Jesus once said:
"Pray so that you won't fall when you are tempted."
Another time he assured us that
"Anything you ask for with faith will be given to you."

And Jesus taught us the Our Father.

Answer the questions.

Why do you think Jesus spoke about prayer so often?

_____

_____

What was the prayer Jesus taught us?

_____

_____

Why did Jesus pray every day?

_____

_____

What do we need to do every day if we want to imitate Jesus?

_____

_____

Jesus prayed every day. By his example he teaches us how important it is for us to pray.

Talking to God, our Father

Do you remember what prayer is?

Fill in the blanks.

needs - God - praise - thanks

Praying is talking with _____, our Father, to_____, him, give him _____, and to present him all our _____.

In the space provided draw the times during the day when you pray.

When you get up in the morning, offering your day to God.

At the beginning of class.

At night, to thank God and to pray for those in need.

Before eating, to thank God for the food and to pray for those who don't have anything to eat.

At Mass we all join together in prayer

As Catholic Christians we go to Mass and are united as we pray together.
Remember that the Church is one big family in which we all have an important role. Through our prayers at Mass, we help each other reach heaven.

God hears our prayers, and thanks to them he helps people all over the world.

Look at the map. See the different people these children are helping through their prayers.

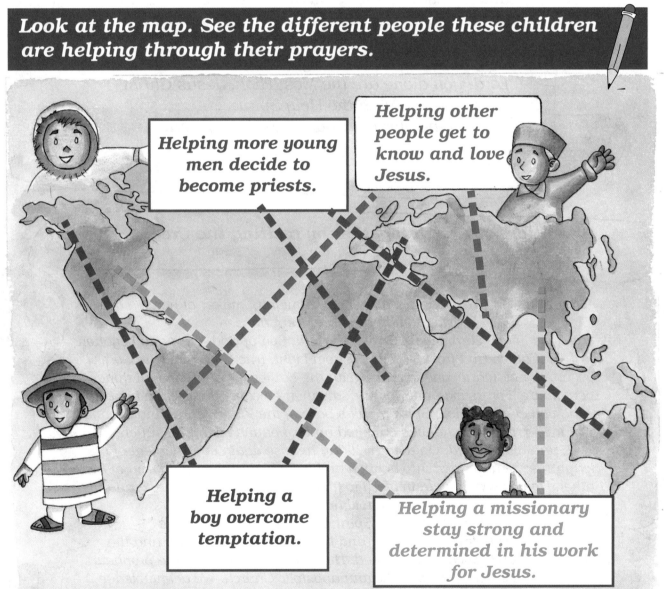

Helping more young men decide to become priests.

Helping other people get to know and love Jesus.

Helping a boy overcome temptation.

Helping a missionary stay strong and determined in his work for Jesus.

This is why it is so important for us to pray together for the needs of all people. God will hear us and always help us.

Prayers of the Mass

These are some of the prayers we say together during Mass.

We praise God together by praying or singing the Gloria...

Glory to God in the highest, and peace to his people on earth. Lord God, Heavenly King, almighty God and Father, we worship you, we give you thanks, we praise you for your glory.
Lord Jesus Christ, only Son of the Father, Lord God, Lamb of God, you take away the sins of the world: have mercy on us; you are seated at the right hand of the Father: receive our prayer.
For you alone are the Holy One, you alone are the Lord, you alone are the Most High, Jesus Christ, with the Holy Spirit, in the glory of God the Father. **Amen.**

We profess our faith together by reciting the Creed...

We believe in One God, the Father, the Almighty, maker of heaven and earth, of all that is seen and unseen.
We believe in one Lord, Jesus Christ, the only Son of God, eternally begotten of the Father, God from God, Light from Light, true God from true God, begotten, not made, one in Being with the Father. Through him all things were made. For us men and for our salvation he came down from heaven: by the power of the Holy Spirit he was born of the Virgin Mary, and became man. For our sake he was crucified under Pontius Pilate; he suffered, died, and was buried. On the third day he rose again in fulfillment of the Scriptures; he ascended into heaven and is seated at the right hand of the Father. He will come again in glory to judge the living and the dead and his kingdom will have no end.
We believe in the Holy Spirit, the Lord, the giver of life, who proceeds from the Father and the Son. With the Father and the Son he is worshipped and glorified. He has spoken through the prophets. We believe in one holy catholic and apostolic Church. We acknowledge one baptism for the forgiveness of sins. We look for the resurrection of the dead, and the life of the world to come. **Amen.**

Complete the crossword puzzle.

1. Less serious sins that are forgiven in communion but can lead us to serious sins.
2. The sacrament Christ instituted at the Last Supper.
3. Receiving Christ under the appearances of bread and wine.
4. Prayer we recite together to profess what we believe.
5. The only thing that can take us away from God.
6. What we need to do for an hour before receiving Communion.

What I have learned

- Jesus teaches us to pray every day.
- During Holy Mass we gather to pray together.
- God hears our prayers.
- By praying together we can help a lot of people get to heaven.

What I will always remember

What is praying?
Praying is talking with God.

Why do we pray?
To praise God, to thank him, and to ask him to help us in all our needs.

What was the prayer Jesus taught us?
The Our Father.

When should we pray?
Always. Not a day should go by without talking to God.

Learn the Creed and the Gloria.

What I am going to do

- During Mass I'm going to pay special attention during the prayers of the faithful, when we pray for the needs of all people.
- I'm also going to pray the Creed and the Gloria with attention and devotion.

Imitating Jesus

Our great friend Jesus taught us apostles many things that we needed to put into practice in our daily lives.

Each one of you should also follow his teachings, living as he lived and as he wants you to live. Then you will always be happy and will reach heaven.

Today we're going to learn how to show Jesus that we are his friends.

Jesus told us

"You are the light of the world"

Jesus said this to show us how we must live and act if we really want to be his friends.

> **Draw a lamp on the table.**

As Jesus' friends, we must follow his teachings and be like lamps that light up the world, helping others reach heaven.

Now draw a lamp under the table.

Answer the questions.

What are lamps for?_____

_____

Which lamp is going to help the children most with their homework?

_____

Which one isn't going to help at all?_____

_____

How can I be the light of the world?

Follow these children as they go through their day. Help them remember what they need to do to be lights to others and true friends of Jesus.

Write on the lines below what Jesus would want the people in each picture to do each step of the way.

If we read Christ's word and live according to his teachings, we will be his true friends and the light of the world.

What I have learned

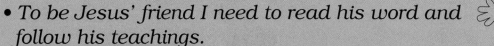

- To be Jesus' friend I need to read his word and follow his teachings.
- I am called to be the light of the world, helping others to be closer to Jesus.
- If I live and act as Jesus has taught me, I will be a light for the world.

What I will always remember

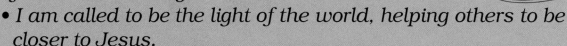

What did Jesus mean when he said that we are the light of the world?
He meant that we must help others get to know him by the way we live.

How can we show Jesus that we are his friends?
By living according to his words and imitating his actions.

What I am going to do

- When I say my morning prayers I'm going to take a moment to think about what I can do during the day to follow Jesus more closely and be a light at home and at school.
- At night when I say my prayers I'm going to think about how well I've lived up to my promise to be a true friend to Jesus.

The Virgin Mary Helps Me

There was another precious gift that Jesus, our Savior, wanted to leave with us apostles, and with all of you, too. He cherished this gift more than any other on earth.

Jesus left us his mother, the Virgin Mary, to help us overcome temptation, to stay in the state of grace and friendship with God, so that one day we can reach heaven.

Today we're going to see that Mary is the mother of God's great family, the Church.

How Mary lived

Do you remember some special moments from Mary's life?

Look at the drawings and write down what you remember about these events in Mary's life.

_____

_____

_____

_____

_____

_____

_____

_____

_____

_____

_____

_____

Draw another event from Mary's life that you remember, and describe that event in the lines below.

_____

_____

Mary and You

The Virgin Mary is your mother. She loves you, takes care of you, and helps you on your way to heaven. She helps you resist temptation and always stay in the state of grace and friendship with God.

Look at the drawings.

In the box write a paragraph about Mary's role in your life.

The Virgin Mary is the Mother of the Church

Mary is also the mother of all God's family, the Church. She looks after us and keeps us united. She is constantly watching over the Church everywhere.

Below are three moments in history when Mary miraculously appeared in different parts of the world to help us and to encourage us to keep striving to love Jesus and reach heaven.

Research the history of each apparition and list some basic facts about it. Draw each one in the box beside it on the lines below.

Our Lady of Guadalupe:

_____

_____

_____

_____

_____

Our Lady of Fatima:

_____

_____

_____

_____

_____

Our Lady of Lourdes:

_____

_____

_____

_____

_____

Mary is present in the Church all over the world at every moment, helping all her children reach heaven.

What I have learned

- Jesus has left us a great gift: his Mother, the Virgin Mary.
- The Virgin Mary is our Mother. She helps us overcome temptation, stay in the state of grace, and reach heaven.
- Mary is the mother of God's great family, the Church.

What I will always remember

Who is the Blessed Virgin Mary?
The Blessed Virgin Mary is the mother of Jesus and our heavenly mother.

Who is the mother of the Church?
The Blessed Virgin Mary is the Mother of the Church.

What I am going to do

- I'm going to take a flower and place it at Mary's feet in the chapel, asking her to help me stay in the state of grace and friendship with God.
- During my morning prayers I'm going to ask Mary, full of love and trust in her, to be with me throughout my day.
- I'm also going to pray to her for my family and friends.

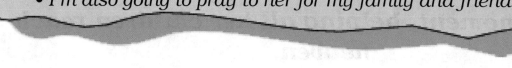

The Holy Rosary

When Jesus went up to heaven to be with his Father, the Blessed Virgin stayed with us apostles to help us and encourage us.

Mary is always with all of you, too. There is a very special way to stay close to her and obtain her help in your lives.

Today we're going to remember how to be very close to Mary, our mother in heaven.

The Holy Rosary

When we pray the Rosary we pray decades of Hail Marys as we meditate on Jesus' life. It is the best way to be close to Mary and obtain her help.

How is the rosary prayed?

1. We begin the rosary with the Apostles' Creed followed by:

- **1 Our Father**
- **2 Hail Marys**
- **3 Glory to the Father**

2. Jesus' life is divided into four sets of "mysteries": the Joyful Mysteries, the Sorrowful Mysteries, the Glorious Mysteries and the Luminous Mysteries. Different mysteries are prayed on different days of the week:

- **Monday & Saturday:** Joyful Mysteries
- **Tuesday & Friday:** Sorrowful Mysteries
- **Wednesday & Sunday:** Glorious Mysteries
- **Thursday:** Luminous Mysteries

3. Each Decade, or Mystery, consists of:

- **1 Our Father**
- **10 Hail Marys**
- **1 Glory to the Father**

As each Hail Mary is prayed we meditate on the Mysteries and talk to Mary, telling her how much we love her.

4. Hail Holy Queen is prayed at the end.

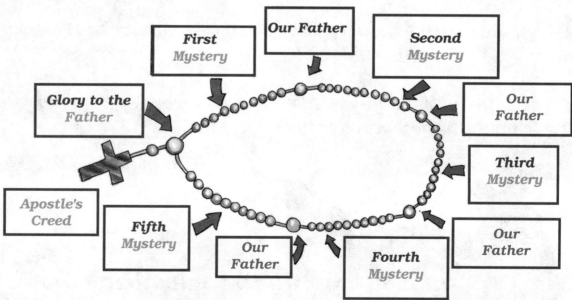

Praying the rosary is like offering Mary ten flowers with each mystery. It's a way of telling her over and over again how much you love her. Pray the rosary every day and the Blessed Virgin will help you reach heaven.

The Joyful Mysteries

These are the mysteries we meditate on when we pray the rosary on Mondays and Saturdays.

Color the pictures and write under each one which mystery it is about.

1st Mystery: The Annunciation
2nd Mystery: The Visitation
3rd Mystery: The Nativity
4th Mystery: The Presentation
5th Mystery: The Finding of the Child Jesus in the Temple

The Sorrowful Mysteries
These Mysteries are prayed on Tuesdays and Fridays.

Color the pictures and write under each one which mystery it is about.

1st Mystery: The Agony in the Garden
2nd Mystery: The Scourging at the Pillar
3rd Mystery: The Crowning of Thorns
4th Mystery: The Carrying of the Cross
5th Mystery: The Crucifixion and Death of Jesus

_____   _____

_____   _____

_____

_____   _____

_____   _____

The Glorious Mysteries

These mysteries are prayed on Wednesdays and Sundays.

Color the pictures and write under each one which mystery it is about.

1st Mystery: The Resurrection
2nd Mystery: The Ascension
3rd Mystery: The Descent of the Holy Spirit on the Apostles
4th Mystery: The Assumption of Mary into heaven
5th Mystery: The Coronation of Mary as Queen of the Universe

The Luminous Mysteries
These mysteries are prayed on Thursdays.

Color the picture and write under each one which mystery it is about.

1st Mystery: John Baptizes Jesus in the Jordam
2nd Mystery: Jesus Reveals His Glory at the Wedding at Cana
3rd Mystery: Jesus Proclaims the Kingdom of God
and Calls Us to Conversion
4th Mystery: The Transfiguration of Jesus
5th Mystery: Jesus Gives Us the Eucharist

_____

_____

_____

_____

What I have learned

- Mary is our mother and she helps us on our way to heaven.
- The best way to stay united to Mary is by praying the Holy Rosary.
- We should pray the Rosary every day with great love and devotion.
- When we pray the Rosary we tell Mary over and over how much we love her.

What I will always remember

What are the main prayers we have for praying to the Blessed Virgin?
The Hail Mary and the rosary.

What is the Holy Rosary?
It is a prayer consisting of decades of the Hail Mary during which we meditate on the mysteries of Jesus' life.

Learn the Hail Holy Queen.

Hail, holy Queen, mother of Mercy,
hail, our life, our sweetness, and our hope.
To you we cry, the children of Eve;
to you we send up our sighs,
mourning and weeping in this land of exile.
Turn, then, most gracious advocate,
your eyes of mercy toward us;
lead us home at last
and show us the blessed fruit of your womb, Jesus:
O clement, O loving, O sweet Virgin Mary.

What I am going to do

- I'm going to pray a mystery, or decade, of the rosary every day. I'm going to invite a friend or one of my brothers or sisters to do the same.

The Liturgy

Jesus once told us apostles that he would always be with us, that he would never leave us on our own. This made us extremely happy because we never wanted to be without him.

Jesus is with all of you, too, in many different ways and throughout the whole year.

Today we're going to learn how to live with Jesus all year long.

All year long

Throughout the year there are different celebrations when you and your family and friends are together.

At these celebrations you remember or mark important days in your life and the life of those you love.

Here are a few of those celebrations.

- **My birthday is on (month & day)** _____
- **My saint's day is on** _____
- **The last day of school is on** _____
- **My father's birthday is on** _____
- **My mother's birthday is on** _____

Draw pictures of two of these celebrations in the box below.

Date:_____
Celebration:_____

Date:_____
Celebration:_____

Just as you have important events and celebrations throughout the year, Jesus has them, too. In this way, he stays with us through the Liturgy.

Jesus is with us

The liturgy has acts of worship where we Catholic Christians praise, glorify, and adore Christ who remains with us in the Church. Thanks to these acts, many people are saved and reach heaven.

These acts of worship are celebrated throughout the year, inviting us to recall the life, death, and resurrection of Christ. This is what we call the "Liturgical Year."

Compare these two calendars:

Calendar year:

**Begins in January.
Ends in December.
Divided into 12 months.
Has 365 days.**

Liturgical year:
**Begins at Advent.
Ends on the Feast of Christ the King.
Divided into 7 Liturgical seasons.
Has 365 days.**

If the sentence relates to the calendar year, fill in the sun; if it relates to the liturgical year, fill in the candle."

 Tells us when the new school year begins.

 Tells us when Holy Week begins.

 Tells you when you have your baseball and soccer games.

 Tells us when to celebrate Pentecost.

The liturgical year

2. The liturgical season of Christmas begins on December 25th, the birth of Jesus, and runs through the Feast of the Epiphany on January 6.

1. The liturgical year begins with the Advent season, the four weeks leading up to Christmas. During Advent we prepare ourselves for living the Christmas season very close to Jesus.

3. After Epiphany, Ordinary Time begins, and here we should also be very close to God.

9. The Liturgical year ends with the Feast of Christ the King.

8. After Pentecost, when the Holy Spirit descends on Mary and the apostles, liturgical Ordinary Time resumes.

4. Lenten Time begins on Ash Wednesday. During Lent we prepare ourselves to live Holy Week and the Easter Season very close to Jesus.

5. Holy Week begins on Palm Sunday. During Holy Week we recall the Last Supper and the Passion, Death, and Resurrection of Our Lord.

7. Forty days after Easter we celebrate the Feast of the Ascension when Jesus ascends to heaven to be with his Father.

6. Easter Season begins on Easter Sunday and lasts until Pentecost. The Easter Season is a time of great rejoicing.

Living with Christ all year long

Underneath each picture write the name of the liturgical time being shown. Also write what you do during that time to live it more deeply.

Advent - Lent - Holy Week - Easter

*Liturgical Time:*_____
*What I do:*_____
_____
_____

*Liturgical Time:*_____
*What I do:*_____
_____
_____

*Liturgical Time:*_____
*What I do:*_____
_____
_____

*Liturgical Time:*_____
*What I do:*_____
_____
_____

Draw a blue line under the correct answer.

What do we do during Advent?
• *Prepare our hearts for Christmas by praying and doing good works.*
• *Prepare our hearts for Holy Week by praying and doing good works.*

What do we do during Lent?
• *Prepare our hearts for Christmas by praying and doing good works.*
• *Prepare our hearts for Holy Week by praying and doing good works.*

What do we recall during Holy Week?
• *The birth of Jesus.*
• *The Passion, Death, and Resurrection of Jesus.*

What do we recall at Christmas?
• *The birth of Jesus.*
• *The Passion, Death, and Resurrection of Jesus.*

How should we live Ordinary Time?
• *With joy and hope.*
• *In no special way, just like any other time of the year.*

How should we celebrate the feasts of the Saints?
• *By getting to know them and striving to imitate them.*
• *Like any other day of the year.*

When is the Easter Candle used?
• *During Advent.*
• *During the Easter Season.*

When does Lent start?
• *On Ash Wednesday.*
• *On the Feast of Christ the King.*

When does the liturgical year end?
• *On the Feast of Christ the King.*
• *On the first Sunday of Advent.*

When does the liturgical year begin?
• *On the Feast of Christ the King.*
• *On the first Sunday of Advent.*

What I have learned

- The liturgy consists of acts of worship through which we adore Christ who remains with us in the Church.
- The liturgical year relives the mysteries of the life, death, and resurrection of Jesus, and celebrates the lives of the saints.
- Salvation history is relived through the liturgical calendar.
- If I carefully follow the liturgical year I will be very close to Christ.

What I will always remember

What is the liturgy?
The liturgy is made up of acts of worship by which we adore Christ who remains with us in the Church.

When does the Church celebrate the mysteries of Christ's life?
It celebrates them throughout the liturgical year.

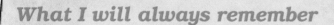

What is the liturgical year?
The liturgical year relives the mysteries of the life, death, and resurrection of Jesus, and celebrates the lives of the saints.

What is relived during the liturgical year?
Salvation history is relived.

What I am going to do

- Every Sunday when I go to Mass I'm going to make sure I'm aware of where we are in the liturgical year so that I can be closer to Jesus.

Special Colors and Vestments

Did you know that you can tell where we are in the liturgical year by looking at the color of the vestments the priest is wearing at Mass?

Do you know what each thing the priest uses at Mass is for? Pay close attention and you'll find out.

Today we're going to see that in the liturgy each season has its own special colors and decorations.

The host that will become the Body of Christ is placed on the paten. The wine that will become His Blood is placed in the chalice. The cruets contain the wine and water used for celebrating Mass.

The corporal is a linen cloth placed in the center of the altar. The hosts and wine that will be consecrated during the Mass are placed on the corporal. The purificator is another linen cloth used by the priest to purify, or clean, the chalice and paten after communion.

The altar candles remind us of the Last Supper and also symbolize Christ as the light of the world. The altar cloth reminds us of the table used at the Last Supper.

The Sacramentary and the Lectionary are the books used during Mass. They contain the liturgy and the Word of God. The sacramentary rests on the altar in its stand, and the lectionary stays on the lectern.

The crucifix reminds us of Jesus' sacrifice on the cross, by which he saved us from sin and opened the way to heaven for us. Jesus is present in the tabernacle in the sacrament of the Eucharist.

The Blessed Virgin is always with us at the celebration of Mass, and throughout our entire lives.

Next to the numbers below, write the name of the object and what it is used for.

1._____

_____

2._____

_____

3._____

_____

4._____

_____

5._____

_____

6._____

_____

Liturgical colors

The priest dresses, or vests, with a chasuble of different colors to say Mass because each color means something.

White
Symbolizes joy and purity. It is used during the Christmas and Easter Seasons.

Green
Symbolizes hope. It is used during Ordinary Time.

Violet
Symbolizes suffering and penance. It is used during Advent, Lent, and Holy Week.

Red
Symbolizes the fire of the Holy Spirit and martyrdom. Used on Pentecost and on the feast days of holy martyrs.

Based on the color of the priest's vestments, write which liturgical time is being celebrated.

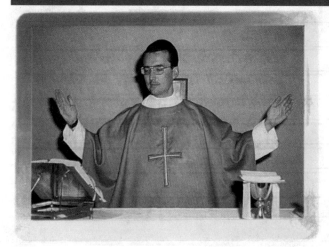

_____ _____

_____ _____

_____ _____

Color the priest's vestment to match the liturgical time of the Mass he is celebrating.

Christmas Day

The first Sunday of Lent

The second Sunday of Ordinary Time

The feast of Sts. Isaac Jogues and Jean de Brébeuf, who died as martyrs of the Faith

What I have learned

- At Mass and in the liturgy different objects, colors, and decorations are used.
- All of these things should be treated with great respect.
- The colors used in the liturgy symbolize things related to the liturgical season being celebrated.

What I will always remember

What does white symbolize in the liturgy?
Joy and purity. It is used during the Christmas and Easter seasons.

What does green symbolize in the liturgy?
Hope. It is used during Ordinary Time.

What does violet symbolize in the liturgy?
Suffering and penance. It is used during Advent, Lent, and Holy Week.

What does red symbolize in the liturgy?
The fire of the Holy Spirit and martyrdom. It is used at Pentecost and on the feast days of holy martyrs.

What I am going to do

- I'm going to pay attention at Mass, aware of what the different colors and decorations represent.
- I'm going to help my friends, brothers, and sisters to pay close attention at Mass.

Sunday is when Christians come together...

When we apostles had something special to celebrate, we got together with Jesus. We were a family and we loved being together.

You, too, as members of God's great family, get together every week to participate in Jesus' celebration.

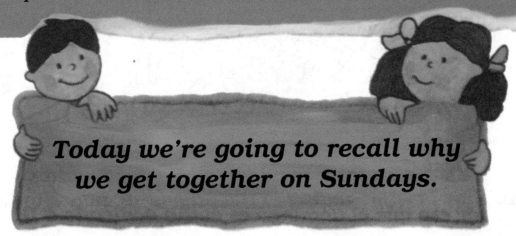

Today we're going to recall why we get together on Sundays.

Easter Sunday

On the Sunday after Jesus died on the cross, Mary Magdalene went to visit the tomb in which Jesus' body had been placed. When she got there, she saw that the stone in front of the tomb had been rolled away. She thought someone had stolen Jesus' body and went running to tell Peter and the other apostles.

**Jesus rose from the dead on Easter Sunday,
and that is why Sunday is the day we dedicate to God.**

Peter and John ran to the tomb and saw that Jesus' body was not there. Then an angel told them Jesus had risen from the dead, just as he said he would.

Color this drawing of the Resurrection of Jesus, our friend and Savior.

On Sundays we remember the Resurrection of Jesus, our friend and Savior.

Sunday is the Lord's day

Sunday is family-reunion day for the Church. We Catholic Christians get together

- **at Jesus' great celebration, the Mass**
- **to pray together**
- **to be united to Christ and each other in Holy Communion**

Sunday is a feast day for Catholic Christians. It should be a very special day for all of us.

Do you remember the Ten Commandments? What was the Third Commandment?

Write it down here:

_____

Now write down some things you can do to keep the Lord's day holy:

_____

_____

Fill in the blanks:

pray - risen - family - feast - Communion - Mass

On Sundays we celebrate the fact that Christ has _____.
Sunday is a _____ day for Christians.
God's _____ gets together on Sundays to celebrate _____.

We Catholic Christians get together on Sundays to _____ together and to receive _____.

Sundays are for God

On Sundays we remember Jesus' Resurrection.
It's a day of rest that should be spent with those we love, putting God and others first.

Draw a blue circle around the things you do on Sundays, and a red circle around the things you do the rest of the week.

In the space provided write what you did last Sunday.

_____

_____

_____

_____

What I have learned

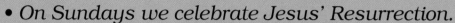

- On Sundays we celebrate Jesus' Resurrection.
- Sunday is a day dedicated to God.
- Sunday is a feast day for Christians.
- On Sunday we Catholic Christians meet to celebrate Mass, pray together, and receive Communion.

What I will always remember:

What day do we dedicate to God?
Sunday.

Why is Sunday the Lord's day?
Because that's the day Jesus rose from the dead.

What I am going to do

- Every Sunday I'm going to take some time to think about God and to thank him for all that he has given me.
- On Sundays I'm going to help out at home as much as I can.